MR. JUSTICE GASELEE

(ORIGINAL OF MR. JUSTICE STARELEIGH).

Sketched by the Editor from the family portrait in the possession of H. Gaselee, Esq.

Bardell v. Pickwick

The Trial for Breach of Promise
of Marriage held at the Guildhall
Sittings, on April 1, 1828, before
Mr. Justice Stareleigh and a Special
Jury of the City of London.

Edited with Notes and Commentaries

by

PERCY FITZGERALD, M.A., F.S.A.

Barrister-at-Law;
and sometime Crown Prosecutor on the North-East Circuit (Ireland).

WITH ILLUSTRATIONS.

THE LAWBOOK EXCHANGE, LTD.
Clark, New Jersey

ISBN-13: 978-1-58477-420-4 (cloth)
ISBN-13: 978-1-61619-045-3 (paperback)

Lawbook Exchange edition 2005, 2010

The quality of this reprint is equivalent to the quality of the original work.

Printed in the United States of America on acid-free paper

THE LAWBOOK EXCHANGE, LTD.
33 Terminal Avenue
Clark, New Jersey 07066-1321

*Please see our website for a selection of our other publications
and fine facsimile reprints of classic works of legal history:*
www.lawbookexchange.com

Library of Congress Cataloging-in-Publication Data

Dickens, Charles, 1812-1870.
    [Pickwick papers. Selections]
Bardell v. Pickwick : the trial for breach of promise of marriage held at the Guildhall
Sittings, on April 1, 1828, before Mr. Justice Starleigh and a special jury of the
City of London / edited with notes and commentaries by Percy Fitzgerald.
    p. cm.
"With illustrations."
ISBN 1-58477-420-7 (cloth : alk. paper)
    1. Trials (Breach of promise) -- Fiction. 2. London (England)--Fiction. I. Fitzgerald,
Percy Hetherington, 1834-1925. II. Title.

PR4569.A3 2004
823'.8--dc22
                                                 200306471

Bardell v. Pickwick

The Trial for Breach of Promise
of Marriage held at the Guildhall
Sittings, on April 1, 1828, before
Mr. Justice Stareleigh and a Special
Jury of the City of London.

Edited with Notes and Commentaries

by

PERCY FITZGERALD, M.A., F.S.A.

Barrister-at-Law;
and sometime Crown Prosecutor on the North-East Circuit (Ireland).

WITH ILLUSTRATIONS.

LONDON

ELLIOT STOCK 62 PATERNOSTER ROW E.C.

1902

CONTENTS.

	Page
Introduction	1
The Cause of Action	4
The Trial	26
The Judge	31
The Court	37
Serjeant Buzfuz	40
The Opening Speech	44
The Incriminating Letters	50
The Plaintiff's Case	54
Winkle's Evidence	61
A Revelation	68
The Defendant's Case	83
Charge and Verdict	93
Plea for " Dodson and Fogg "	101
The Cognovit	108
Release from the Fleet	114

ILLUSTRATIONS.

	Page
Mr. Justice Gaselee - - - -	*Frontispiece*
The Cause of Action - - - - -	7
Mr. Pickwick expounds his Case to his Counsel -	22
Serjeant Snubbin, K.C. - - - - -	24
Exterior of the Guildhall Court.—Now City Museum - - - - - - -	26
Interior of the Guildhall Court - - -	27
Serjeant Buzfuz, K.C. - - - - -	40
Mr. Pickwick as a Monster - - - -	47
Mr. Skimpin - - - - - - -	61
Mr. Phunky - - - - - - -	68
The Double Bedded Room, Great White Horse, Ipswich - - - - - - -	75

BARDELL VERSUS PICKWICK.

INTRODUCTION.

There are few things more familiar or more interesting to the public than this *cause célèbre*. It is better known than many a real case: for every one knows the Judge, his name and remarks—also the Counsel—(notably Sergeant Buzfuz)—the witnessess, and what they said— and of course all about the Plaintiff and the famous Defendant. It was tried over seventy years ago at "the Guildhall Settens," and was described by Boz some sixty-three years ago. Yet every detail seems fresh— and as fresh as ever. It is astonishing that a purely technical sketch like this, whose humours might be relished only by such specialists as Barristers and Attorneys, who would understand the jokes levelled at the Profession, should be so well understanded of the people. All see the point of the legal satire. It is a quite a prodigy. Boz had the art, in an extraordinary degree, of thus vividly commending trade processes, professional allusions, and methods to outsiders, and making them humourous and intelligible. Witness Jackson, when he came to "serve" Mr. Pickwick and friends with the *subpœnas*. It is a dry, business-like process, but how racy Boz made it. A joke sparkles in every line.

This trial for Breach has been debated over and over

B

again among lawyers and barristers, some contending
that "there was no evidence at all to go to the Jury"
as to a promise; others insisting on mis-direction, and
that there was evidence that ought not to have been
admitted. The law has since been changed, and by
later Acts both Mrs. Bardell and Mr. Pickwick would
have been allowed to tell their stories and to have been
cross-examined. Mrs. Bardell was almost justified in
supposing that Mr. Pickwick was offering his hand when
he was merely speaking of engaging a man-servant.
But then the whole would have been spoiled. Under
the present systems, this would all have come out. Mr.
Pickwick, when it came to his turn, would have explained what his proceedings meant. It is a most
perfect and vivid satire on the hackneyed methods of
the lawyers when dealing with the witnesses. Nothing
can be more natural or more graphic. It is maintained
to something between the level of comedy and farce:
nor is there the least exaggeration. It applies new as
it did then, though not to the same topics. A hectoring, bullying Counsel, threatening and cruel, would
interfere with the pleasant tone of the play; but it is
all the same conveyed. There is a likeness to Bardell
v. Pickwick in another Burlesque case, tried in our day,
the well-known "Trial by Jury," the joint work of Mr.
Gilbert and the late Sir Arthur Sullivan. The general
tone of both is the same and in the modern work there
is a general Pickwickian flavour. Sir Arthur's music,
too, is highly "Pickwickian," and the joint effort of the
two humorists is infinitely diverting. The Judge is
something of a Stareleigh.

The truth is that Boz, the engenderer of these
facetiæ, apart from his literary gift, was one of the
most brilliant, capable young fellows of his generation.
Whatever he did, he did in the best way, and in the
brightest way. But his power of observation and of

seeing what might be termed the humorous *quiddity* of anything, was extraordinary.

To put absurdity in a proper view for satirical purposes, it has to be generalised from a number of instances, familiar to all. Those legal oddities, the public had seen over and over again, but they had passed unnoticed till this clever observer set to work and noted them. As I say, it required a deep knowledge of the law to set these things in a grotesque light.

Boz had been a sort of general reporter on the *Chronicle :* he "took" everything. He had reported at police courts as well as at the law courts. His quick and bright intelligence seized the humours here, as it did those of the street. He later reported in the Gallery, and was dispatched across country in post-chaises to "take" eminent political speakers—always winning the hearty commendation of his employers for his zeal and energy.

THE CAUSE OF ACTION.

Mr. Pickwick was a well-to-do bachelor, who lived by himself near the city, where he had been in trade. His age was about fifty, as can be accurately calculated by his remark on the sliding at Manor Farm. "I used to do so on the gutters when I was a boy . . . but I hav'nt done such a thing these thirty years." This was said in 1828. He resided in Goswell Street—now Goswell Road—with a widow lady, whose husband had been in the Excise. He cannot have paid more than a pound a week, if so much, for two rooms on the first floor. There was no servant, and the hardworking landlady, Mrs. Martha Bardell, performed all the duties of her household single-handed. As her Counsel later described it,—and see all she did for him!—"She waited on him, attended to his comforts, cooked his meals, looked out his linen for the washer-woman when it went abroad, darned, aired, and prepared it for his wear when it came home, and, in short, enjoyed his fullest trust and confidence." Thus Sergeant Buzfuz, duly "instructed." Not only was there Mr. Pickwick, but there was another lodger, and her little boy Tommy. The worthy woman took care of and looked after all three. This might incline us to take a favorable view of her. She regarded her lodger with feelings of veneration and attachment, of which proof is found in her later talk with Sam. To him she said that " he had always behaved himself like a perfect gentlemen," and then added this significant speech : " It's a terrible thing to be dragged in this

way before the public, but *I now see* that it's the only
thing that I ought to do." That is, she seems to have
held out as long as possible, believing that her amiable
lodger would act as a perfect gentlemen and like himself. But when she found that even an action had no
terrors for him, she saw that there was nothing else
to do but to let the action go on.

And what was Mrs. Bardell like? One would imagine
her a plump, buxom widow, " fat, fair, and forty," with
her dear little boy, " the only pledge of her deceased
exciseman," or say something between thirty and forty
years old. Fortunately, two portraits have come down
to us of the lady—one somewhat of this pattern, and
depicting her, as she flung herself on Mr. Pickwick on
that disastrous morning: the other—a swollen, dreadful
thing, which must be a caricature of the literal presentment. Here we see a woman of gross, enormous
proportions seated on the front bench and apparently
weighing some thirteen or fourteen stone, with a vast
coarse face. This is surely an unfair presentment of
the worthy landlady ; besides, Dodson and Fogg were
too astute practitioners to imperil their chances by exhibiting to his Lordship and the Jury so ill-favoured a
plaintiff. Indeed, we are told that they arranged a
rather theatrical exhibition in this scene, with a view of
creating an impression in their favour.

Many find pleasure in reading the Bookseller's Cata-
logues, and a vast number are showered on me in the
course of the year. But on one of these I always gaze
with a special interest, and even tenderness. For it
comes from one Herbert, who lives in Goswell Road.
Only think, *Goswell* Road—erst Goswell Street, where
just seventy years ago Mrs. Bardell was letting lodgings
and Mr. Pickwick himself was lodging : and on the
cover I read, a furthur attraction, " Goswell Road, near
the 'Angel,'" whence the " stage" which took the party

to the " Spaniard " at Hampstead started ! Sometimes
I am drawn to the shop, crowded with books ; but one's
thoughts stray away from the books into speculations as
to *which* house it was.   But the indications are most
vague, though the eye settles on a decent range of
shabby-looking faded tenements—two storeys high only
—and which *look* like lodging houses.   Some ingenious
commentators have indeed ventured to identify the
house itself, arguing from the very general description
in the text.

We should note, however, Mr. Pickwick's lack of
caution.   He came in the very next day, having apparently made no enquiries as to the landlady.   Had he
done so, he would have learned of the drunken exciseman who met his death by being knocked on the head
with a quart pot.   He might have heard of the friends,
Cluppins, Raddle, etc., who seemed to have been char-
women or something of the sort ; also that there was a
sort of working man as a fellow lodger.   Above all, that
there was no servant in the house.   All which boded ill,
and made it likely that Mr. Pickwick would be the easy
victim of some crafty scheme.

All went well until the unluckly morning in July,
1827, when Mr. Pickwick's friends, coming to pay a
morning call, and entering unexpectedly, surprised Mr.
Pickwick with his landlady fainting in his arms in an
hysterical condition.   This was a very awkward business.   The delinquent, however, did not at once grasp
the situation, and could not " make head or tail of it, or
what the lady meant."   His friends, however, had their
doubts :

" ' What *is* the matter ? ' said the three tongue-tied
Pickwickians.

' I don't know,' replied Mr. Pickwick, pettishly.
' Now, help me, lead this woman down stairs.'

' Oh, I am better now,' said Mrs. Bardell, faintly.

'Let me lead you downstairs,' said the ever gallant Mr. Tupman.

'Thank you, sir—thank you?' exclaimed Mrs. Bardell, hysterically. And dowstairs she was led accordingly, accompanied by her affectionate son.

THE CAUSE OF ACTION.

'I cannot conceive—' said Mr. Pickwick, when his friend returned—'I cannot conceive what has been the matter with that woman. I had merely announced to her my intention of keeping a man servant, when she fell into the extraordinary paroxysm in which you found her. Very extraordinary thing.'

'Very,' said his three friends.

' Placed me in such an extremely awkward situation,'
continued Mr. Pickwick.

' Very,' was the reply of his followers, as they coughed
slightly, and looked dubiously at each other.

This behaviour was not lost upon Mr. Pickwick. He
remarked their incredulity. They evidently suspected
him."

It may be reasonably supposed that Mr. Pickwick had
not been very discreet, or sufficiently cautious in his
general behaviour to his landlady. As we know, he was
rather too effusive in his relations with the fair sex.
One of his weaknesses was *kissing*. He would kiss everybody who was young or good-looking. His maxim was
" Kiss early and kiss often." Who can forget his *systematic* method of greeting the engaging Arabella?
" He (1) took off his spectacles, (2) in great haste, and
(3) taking both the young lady's hands in his (4) kissed
her (5) a great many times (6) perhaps a greater number
of times than was absolutely necessary." Old rogue!
I have little doubt that on his return home from his
tours he encircled the buxom figure of Mrs. Bardell
—all of course in his own paternal and privileged
way.

It should be borne in mind also that Mr. Pickwick was
almost invariably drawn into his more serious scrapes
and embarrassments by this devotion to the sex. The
night in the boarding school garden—the affair with the
spinster lady—his interview with Arabella from the top
of the wall—his devotion to Mrs. Pott and Mrs. Dow-
ler—and much more that we do not hear of, show that
he was a gallant elderly gentleman. Oh, he was a "sly
dog, he was."

There is a curious burst of Mr. Pickwick's which seems
to hint at a sort of tender appreciation on his side.
When the notice of trial was sent to him, in his first ve-
hemence, he broke out that Mrs. Bardell had nothing

to do with the business, " *She hadn't the heart to do it.*"
Mr. Pickwick could not speak with this certainty, unless
he knew the lady's feelings pretty well. *Why* hadn't she
the heart to do it ? Because she was sincerely attached
to him and his interests and was "a dear creature."
This, however, was a fond delusion of the worthy gentleman's. Persons of her class are not quite so disinter-
ested as they appear to be, especially if they have to
interpret the various paternal and comforting advances
made to them by their well to do lodgers.

There is another factor which can hardly be left out,
when considering Mr. Pickwick's responsibility—that is,
his too frequent indulgence in liquor, and the insuffi-
ciency of his head to stand its influence. Now this was
a very important day for him, the first time he was to
set up a man servant. He had to break it to his landlady, who would naturally resent the change. He may
have been *priming* himself with some of those perpetual
glasses of brandy and water to which he was addicted,
and who knows but that, in his ardour to propitiate,
he may have gone a *little* too far ? This fact too, of
the introducing a man servant into her establishment,
Mrs. Bardell may have indistinctly associated with a
general change in his life. If she were to become Mrs.
Pickwick her duties might be naturally expected to
devolve on a male assistant.

Next morning he and his friends quitted London on
their travels to Eatanswill in pursuit of adventure. He
airily dismissed the matter. We may wonder whether
he made any remonstrance to his landlady before his
departure. Probably he did not, fancying that she had
been merely in a slight fit of the "tantrums."

At Bury, however, after the boarding-school adventure, he was to be painfully awakened. He was sitting
with his friends after dinner at the "Angel," in his
happiest mood. Winkle had related his quarrel with

Pott *in re* Mrs. Pott, in a humorous fashion when one of the most delightful of humorous scenes followed.

Mr. Pickwick was proceeding with his scathing re- buke. when Sam enters with a letter.

" ' I don't know this hand,' said Mr. Pickwick, opening the letter. ' Mercy on us ! what's this ? It must be a jest ; it—it—can't be true.'

' What's the matter ? ' was the general inquiry.

' Nobody dead, is there ? ' said Wardle, alarmed at the horror in Mr. Pickwick's countenance.

" Mr. Pickwick made no reply, but, pushing the letter across the table, and desiring Mr. Tupman to read it aloud, fell back in his chair with a look of vacant as- tonishment quite alarming to behold.

" Mr. Tupman, with a trembling voice, read the letter, of which the following is a copy :—

> ' *Freeman's Court, Cornhill, August 28th, 1827.*
> *Bardell against Pickwick.*

Sir,

> *Having been instructed by Mrs. Martha Bardell to commence an action against you for a breach of promise of marriage, for which the plaintiff lays her damages at fifteen hundred pounds, we beg to inform you that a writ has been issued against you in this suit in the Court of Common Pleas ; and request to know, by return of post, the name of your attorney in London, who will accept service thereof.*

> > *We are, Sir,*
> > *Your obedient servants,*
> > *DODSON & FOGG.*

Mr. Samuel Pickwick.' "

So Mr. Pickwick, the general mentor, the philoso- pher and friend—the man of high moral tone, " born to set the world aright"—the general lecturer of his " followers," was now in for an action at law of the most awkward and unpleasant kind. To be philandering with one's landlady! rather low form this. But what would they say down at Manor Farm? How Isabella Wardle and her sister—and all the girls—would laugh! And the spinster aunt—*she* would enjoy it! But there was no help for it. It must be faced.

Naturally Mr. Pickwick felt uncomfortable, and his first idea was to arrange the matter. This was a sensible course, and he ought at once to have put the matter into the hands of his friend Perker, with full powers to treat. But no. Mr. Pickwick's vanity and indiscretion made him meddle in the business behind his solicitor's back, as it where, and with damaging results to himself—a warning to all such amateurs. It must be said that Dodson and Fogg's behaviour at the extraordinary visit which he paid them was marked by a certain propriety. Mr. Pickwick insisted on knowing what were the grounds of action—that is, the details of the evidence against him—in short, their case. They, very correctly, refused to tell him. "The case may be false or it may be true—it may be credible it may be incredible." But all the same it was a strong case. This was as much as they could tell. Mr. Pickwick could only urge that if "it were so, he was a most unfortunate man," on which Dodson promptly—"I hope you are, sir, I trust you may be, sir. If you are really innocent, you are more unfortunate than I had believed any man could possibly be."

Mr. Pickwick then rather foolishly asked did he understand they meant to go on with the action—as if they could have been affected by his declaration. "Understand?" was the reply, "that you certainly may"—a very natural speech.

With some want of professional delicacy and etiquette, Dodson seized the opportunity to "serve" Mr. Pickwick; but they were not a high-class firm and their methods were not high-class. Then an extraordinarily

incredible display followed. His passion broke forth.
*" Of all the disgraceful and rascally proceedings he ever,
etc. ! "* Dodson summoned his clerks to listen to this
gross language, and said, " Perhaps you would like to
call us swindlers." *" You are,"* said Mr. Pickwick.
Fogg even wished him to assault them—and perhaps
he would have done so, but for Sam, who at last got
him away. This was certainly not correct, but how
aggravating was Mr. Pickwick ! One is rather astonished at the forbearance of this sharp firm.

Now, had Mr. Pickwick gone straight to his lodgings
in Goswell Street and seen Mrs. Bardell, heard her views
and claims, had he been told by her that she had been
professionally urged to go to law as she had such a
strong case—there might have been some excuse for this
violence to Dodson and Fogg. But he knew nothing
whatever of the matter—knew nothing of the attornies
—and in his blind fury gratuitously assumed that they
had " conspired " to harass him in this way. True, he
had overheard how they had treated poor Ramsey.

This very *malapropos* visit of Mr. Pickwick to the
firm was, as I said, a mistake and damaged his case.
It showed that he was nervous and anxious, and *insecure.*
He took nothing by it. There was in truth much
short-sighted cunning in his ways, which came of his
overweening vanity. But this was only one of several
attempts he made to worm out something to his own
advantage.

Another of Mr. Pickwick's foolish manœuvres was
his sending his man to his old lodgings to his landlady
—ostensibly to fetch away his " things," when this dialogue passed :

" ' Tell Mrs. Bardell she may put a bill up, as soon as
she likes.'

' Wery good, sir,' replied Mr. Weller ; ' anythin'
more, sir.'

'Nothing more, Sam.'

" Mr. Weller stepped slowly to the door, as if he expected something more ; slowly opened it, slowly stepped out, and had slowly closed it within a couple of inches, when Mr. Pickwick called out.

'Sam.'

'Sir,' said Mr. Weller, stepping quickly back, and closing the door behind him.

'I have no objection, Sam, to your endeavouring to ascertain how Mrs. Bardell herself seems disposed towards me, and whether it is really probable that this vile and groundless action is to be carried to extremity. *I say, I do not object to your doing this, if you wish it, Sam,*' said Mr. Pickwick. Sam gave a short nod of intelligence and left the room."

Now this was very artful on the part of Mr. Pickwick, but it was a very shallow sort of artfulness, and it was later to recoil on himself. Sam of course saw through it at once. It never dawned on this simple-minded man what use the Plaintiff's solicitors would make of his *demarche.*

When the subœnas were served he rushed off to Perker :

" 'They have subpœna'd my servant too,' said Mr. Pickwick.

'Sam ? ' said Perker.

Mr. Pickwick replied in the affirmative.

'Of course, my dear sir ; of course. I knew they would. I could have told *you* that a month ago. You know, my dear sir, if you *will* take the management of your affairs into your own hands after intrusting them to your solicitor, you must also take the consequences.' Here Mr. Perker drew himself up with conscious dignity, and brushed some stray grains of snuff from his shirt frill.

'And what do they want him to prove?' asked Mr. Pickwick, after two or three minutes' silence.

'That ·you sent him up to the plaintiff's to make some offer of a compromise, I suppose,' replied Perker. 'It don't matter much, though; I don't think many counsel could get a great deal out of *him*.'

'I don't think they could,' said Mr. Pickwick."

The minutiæ of legal process are prosaic and uninteresting, and it might seem impossible to invest them with any dramatic interest; but how admirably has Boz lightened up and coloured the simple incident of an attorney's clerk—a common, vulgar fellow of the lowest type, arriving to serve his subpœnas on the witnesses—all assumed to be hostile. The scene is full of touches of light comedy.

"'How de do, sir?' said Mr. Jackson, nodding to Mr. Pickwick.

"That gentlemen bowed, and looked somewhat surprised for the physiognomy of Mr. Jackson dwelt not in his recollection.

'I have called from Dodson and Fogg's,' said Mr. Jackson, in an explanatory tone.

"Mr. Pickwick roused at the name. 'I refer you to my attorney, sir: Mr. Perker, of Gray's Inn,' said he. 'Waiter, show this gentleman out.'

'Beg your pardon, Mr. Pickwick,' said Jackson, deliberately depositing his hat on the floor, and drawing from his pocket the strip of parchment. 'But personal service, by clerk or agent, in these cases, you know, Mr. Pickwick—nothing like caution, sir, in all legal forms?'

"Here Mr. Jackson cast his eye on the parchment; and, resting his hands on the table, and looking round with a winning and persuasive, smile, said: 'Now, come; don't let's have no words about such a little matter as this. Which of you gentlemen's name's Snodgrass?'

"At this inquiry Mr. Snodgrass gave such a very undisguised and palpable start, that no further reply was needed.

'Ah! I thought so,' said Mr. Jackson, more affably than before. 'I've got a little something to trouble you with, sir.'

'Me!' exclaimed Mr. Snodgrass.

'It's only a *subpœna* in Bardell and Pickwick on behalf of the plaintiff,' replied Jackson, singling out one of the slips of paper, and producing a shilling from his waistcoat pocket. 'It'll come on, in the settens after Term; fourteenth of Febooary, we expect; we've marked it a special jury cause, and it's only ten down the paper. That's yours, Mr. Snodgrass.' As Jackson said this he presented the parchment before the eyes of Mr. Snodgrass, and slipped the paper and the shilling into his hand.

" Mr. Tupman had witnessed this process in silent astonishment, when Jackson, turning sharply upon him, said :

'I think I ain't mistaken when I say your name's Tupman, am I ? '

" Mr. Tupman looked at Mr. Pickwick ; but, perceiving no encouragement in that gentleman's widely-opened eyes to deny his name, said :

'Yes, my name *is* Tupman, sir.'

'And that other gentleman's Mr. Winkle, I think ? ' said Jackson.

" Mr. Winkle faltered out a reply in the affirmative ; and both gentlemen were forthwith invested with a slip of paper, and a shilling each, by the dexterous Mr. Jackson.

'Now," said Jackson, 'I'm affraid you'll think me rather troublesome, but I want somebody else, if it ain't inconvenient. I *have* Samuel Weller's name here, Mr. Pickwick.'

'Send my servant here, waiter,' said Mr. Pickwick.

The waiter retired, considerably astonished, and Mr. Pickwick motioned Jackson to a seat.

" There was a painful pause, which was at length broken by the innocent defendant.

'I suppose, sir,' said Mr. Pickwick, his indignation rising while he spoke; 'I suppose, sir, that it is the intention of your employers to seek to criminate me upon the testimony of my own friends ? '

" Mr. Jackson struck his forefinger several times against the left side of his nose, to intimate that he was not there to disclose the secrets of the prison-house, and playfully rejoined :

' Not knowin', can't say.'

' For what other reason, sir,' pursued Mr. Pickwick, ' are these subpœnas served upon them, if not for this ? '

' Very good plant, Mr. Pickwick,' replied Jackson, slowly shaking his head. ' But it won't do. No harm in trying, but there's little to be got out of me.'

" Here Mr. Jackson smiled once more upon the company, and, applying his left thumb to the tip of his nose, worked a visionary coffee-mill with his right hand : thereby performing a very graceful piece of pantomime (then much in vogue, but now, unhappily, almost obsolete) which was familiarly denominated ' taking a grinder.' (Imagine a modern solicitor's clerk " Taking a grinder ! ")

' No, no, Mr. Pickwick,' said Jackson, in conclusion ; ' Perker's people must guess what we served these subpœnas for. If they can't, they must wait till the action comes on, and then they'll find out.'

" Mr. Pickwick bestowed a look of excessive disgust on his unwelcome visitor, and would probably have hurled some tremendous anathema at the heads of Messrs. Dodson and Fogg, had not Sam's entrance at the instant interrupted him.

' Samuel Weller ? ' said Mr. Jackson, inquiringly.

'Vun o' the truest things as you've said for many a long year,' replied Sam, in a most composed manner.

'Here's a subpœna for you, Mr. Weller,' said Jackson.

'What's that in English?' inquired Sam.

'Here's the original,' said Jackson, declining the required explanation.

'Which?' said Sam.

'This,' replied Jackson, shaking the parchment.

'Oh, that's the 'rig'nal, is it?' said Sam. 'Well, I'm wery glad I've seen the 'rig'nal, 'cos it's a gratifyin' sort o' thing, and eases vun's mind so much.'

'And here's the shilling,' said Jackson. 'It's from Dodson and Fogg's.'

'And it's uncommon handsome o' Dodson and Fogg, as knows so little of me, to come down vith a present,' said Sam. 'I feel it as a wery high compliment, sir; it's a wery hon'rable thing to them, as they knows how to reward merit werever they meets it. Besides wich, it's affectin to one's feelin's.'

" As Mr. Weller said this, he inflicted a little friction on his right eye-lid, with the sleeve of his coat, after the most approved manner of actors when they are in domestic pathetics.

" Mr. Jackson seemed rather puzzled by Sam's proceedings; but, as he had served the subpœnas, and had nothing more to say, he made a feint of putting on the one glove which he usually carried in his hand, for the sake of appearances; and returned to the office to report progress."

Another of Mr. Pickwick's foolish and self-willed proceedings was the interview with Serjeant Snubbin, which he so positively insisted upon. We may wonder now-a-days would any K.C. of position have condescended to allow such a proceeding? I fancy it would be thought "irregular:" though perhaps *ex gratia*, and from the oddity of the proposal, it might be conceded.

c

When Mr. Pickwick called upon him, it turned out
that the Serjeant knew nothing whatever of his case;
probably cared nothing about it. It was not in his
line.   He perhaps wondered why the old-fashioned lawyer had "retained" him.   We learn Perker's reason:

'"Well, we've done everything that's necessary.   I
have engaged Serjeant Snubbin.'

'Is he a good man?' inquired Mr. Pickwick.

'Good man!' replied Perker; 'bless your heart and
soul, my dear sir, Serjeant Snubbin is at the very top
of his profession.   Gets treble the business of any man
in court—engaged in every case.   You needn't mention
it abroad; but we say—we of the profession—that
Serjeant Snubbin leads the court by the nose.'"

How foolish was this reasoning can be seen on an instant's reflection.   To "lead the court by the nose" is
well enough in an argument before a judge: but here it
was more important to lead *a jury* by the nose, which
Buzfuz knew how to do.   Moreover when a counsel has
has this power, it usually operates on a special judge
and his colleagues; but who could guarantee that Snubbin's special judge would try the case.   As it turned
out, the Chief Justice fell sick before the day, and Mr.
Justice Stareleigh unexpectedly took the case.   He as
it proved was anything but "led by the nose."   Perker
indeed, summed up the whole weakness of the case in a
single sentence:

"'They have subpoena'd my three friends,' said Mr.
Pickwick.

'Ah! of course they would,' replied Perker.   'Important witnesses; saw you in a delicate situation.'

'But she fainted of her own accord,' said Mr. Pickwick.   'She threw herself into my arms.'

'Very likely, my dear sir,' replied Perker; 'very likely
and very natural.   Nothing more so, my dear sir,
nothing.   *But who's to prove it?*'"

A suggestion, we are told, that rather " staggered "
Mr. Pickwick.

Within ten minutes after he had received the assurance that the thing was impossible, he was conducted
by his solicitors into the outer office of the great Serjeant Snubbin himself.

" It was an uncarpeted room of tolerable dimensions,
with a large writing table drawn up near the fire, the
baize top of which had long since lost all claim to its
original hue of green, and had gradually grown grey
with dust and age, except where all traces of its natural
colour were obliterated by ink-stains.   Upon the table
were numerous little bundles of papers tied with red
tape; and behind it, sat an elderly clerk, whose sleek
appearance and heavy gold watch-chain presented imposing indications of the extensive and lucrative practice
of Mr. Serjeant Snubbin.

' Is the Serjeant in his room, Mr. Mallard?' inquired
Perker, offering his box with all imaginable courtesy.

' Yes, he is,' was the reply, ' but he's very busy.   Look
here; not an opinion given yet, on any one of these
cases; and an expedition fee paid with all of them.'
The clerk smiled as he said this, and inhaled the pinch
of snuff with a zest which seemed to be compounded of
a fondness for snuff and a relish for fees.

' Something like practice that,' said Perker.

' Yes,' said the barrister's clerk, producing his own
box, and offering it with the greatest cordiality; ' and
the best of it is, that as nobody alive except myself can
read the Serjeant's writing, they are obliged to wait for
the opinions, when he has given them, till I have copied
'em, ha—ha—ha !'

' Which makes good for we know who, besides the
Serjeant, and draws a little more out of his clients, eh?'
said Perker; ' Ha, ha, ha !'   At this the Serjeant's
clerk laughed again—not a noisy boisterous laugh, but

a silent, internal chuckle, which Mr. Pickwick disliked
to hear. When a man bleeds inwardly, it is a dangerous
thing for himself; but when he laughs inwardly, it bodes
no good to other people.

'You haven't made me out that little list of the fees
that I'm in your debt, have you?' said Perker.

'No, I have not,' replied the clerk.

'I wish you would,' said Perker. 'Let me have them,
and I'll send you a cheque. But I suppose you're too
busy pocketing the ready money, to think of the debtors,
eh? ha, ha, ha!' This sally seemed to tickle the clerk,
amazingly, and he once more enjoyed a little quiet
laugh to himself.

'But, Mr. Mallard, my dear friend,' said Perker,
suddenly recovering his gravity, and drawing the great
man's great man into a corner, by the lappel of his coat,
'you must persuade the Serjeant to see me, and my
client here.'

'Come, come,' said the clerk, 'that's not bad either.
See the Serjeant! come, that's too absurd." Notwithstanding the absurdity of the proposal, however, the
clerk allowed himself to be gently drawn beyond the
hearing of Mr. Pickwick; and after a short conversation conducted in whispers, walked softly down a little
dark passage and disappeared into the legal luminary's
sanctum, from whence he shortly returned on tiptoe,
and informed Mr. Perker and Mr. Pickwick that the
Serjeant had been prevailed upon, in violation of all his
established rules and customs, to admit them at once.

"The Serjeant was writing when his clients entered;
he bowed abstractedly when Mr. Pickwick was introduced by his solicitor; and then, motioning them to a
seat, put his pen carefully in the inkstand, nursed his
left leg, and waited to be spoken to.

'Mr. Pickwick is the defendant in Bardell and Pickwick, Serjeant Snubbin,' said Perker.

' You are, Sir,' replied Perker.

The Serjeant nodded his head, and waited for something else.

' Mr. Pickwick was anxious to call upon you, Serjeant Snubbin,' said Perker, ' to state to you, before you entered upon the case, that he denies there being any ground or pretence whatever for the action against him; and that unless he came into court with clean hands, and without the most conscientious conviction that he was right in resisting the plaintiff's demand, he would not be there at all. I believe I state your views correctly; do I not, my dear Sir?' said the little man, turning to Mr. Pickwick.

' Quite so,' replied that gentleman.

" Mr. Serjeant Snubbin unfolded his glasses, raised them to his eyes; and, after looking at Mr. Pickwick for a few seconds with great curiosity, turned to Mr. Perker, and said, smiling slightly as he spoke—

' Has Mr. Pickwick a strong case?'

The attorney shrugged his shoulders.

' Do you purpose calling witnesses?'

' No.'

" The smile on the Serjeant's countenance became more defined; he rocked his leg with increased violence, and, throwing himself back in his easy-chair, coughed dubiously.

" These tokens of the Serjeant's presentiments on the subject, slight as they were, were not lost on Mr. Pickwick. He settled the spectacles, through which he had attentively regarded such demonstrations of the barrister's feeling as he had permitted himself to exhibit, more firmly on his nose; and said with great energy, and in utter disregard of all Mr. Perker's admonitory winkings and frownings—

' My wishing to wait upon you for such a purpose as this, Sir, appears, I have no doubt, to a gentleman who sees so much of these matters as you must necessarily do, a very extraordinary circumstance.'

" 'The Serjeant tried to look gravely at the fire, but the smile came back again.

MR. PICKWICK EXPOUNDS HIS CASE TO HIS COUNSEL.

'Gentlemen of your profession, Sir,' continued Mr. Pickwick, 'see the worst side of human nature—all its disputes, all its ill-will and bad blood, rise up before you. You know from your experience of juries (I mean no disparagement to you or them) how much depends upon *effect*; and you are apt to attribute to others, a desire to use, for purposes of deception and self-interest, the very instruments which you, in pure honesty and honour of purpose, and with a laudable desire to do your utmost for your client, know the temper and worth of so well, from constantly employing them yourselves. I really believe that to this circumstance may be attributed the vulgar but very general notion of your being, as a body, suspicious, distrustful, and over-cautious. Conscious as I am, Sir, of the disadvantage of making such a declaration to you, under such circumstances, I have come here, because I wish you distinctly to understand, as my friend Mr. Perker has said, that I am innocent of the falsehood laid to my charge; and although I am very well aware of the inestimable value of your assistance, Sir, I must beg to add, that unless you sincerely believe this, I would rather be deprived of the aid of your talents than have the advantage of them.'

"Long before the close of this address, which we are bound to say was of a very prosy character for Mr. Pickwick, the Serjeant had relapsed into a state of abstraction."

Now the Serjeant might at once have replied to all this, that the innocence or guilt of a client had nothing to do with him, that his use was merely to secure a client such benefit and advantage as the law entitled him to: that a judge and jury would decide the point of innocence. Boz himself evidently shared this popular delusion, and seems to be speaking by Mr. Pickwick's mouth. The sagacious Serjeant, however, took no notice whatever of the appeal, but simply asked "who was with him" in the case. Mr. Phunky was sent for, and asked by his leader "to take Mr. Pickwick away" and "hear anything he may wish to communicate." The party was then bowed out.

The truth was, Mr. Pickwick's attorney was too muc--

of a social character and of the "old family solicitor" pattern for so critical a case. The counsel he "instructed" were unsuitable. Serjeant Snubbin was an overworked "Chamber lawyer," whose whole time and experience was given to furnishing "opinions" on tangled cases; so pressed was he that he took "expedition fees" to give certain cases priority: an illegitimate practice that now the Bar Committee would scarcely tolerate. What could such a man know of nisi prius trials, of cross-examining or handling witnesses? It is enough to give his portrait, as supplied by the author:

SERJEANT SNUBBIN, K.C.

"Mr. Serjeant Snubbin was a lantern-faced, sallow-complexioned man, of about five-and-forty, or—as the novels say—he might be fifty. He had that *dull-looking boiled eye* which is often to be seen in the heads of people who have applied themselves during many years to a weary and laborious course of study; and which would have been sufficient, without the additional eye-glass which dangled from a broad black riband round his neck, to warn a stranger that he was very near-sighted. His hair was thin and weak, which was partly attributable to his having never devoted much time to its arrangement, and partly to his having worn for five-and-twenty

years the forsenic wig which hung on a block beside
him. The marks of hair powder on his coat collar, and
the ill-washed and worse tied white neckerchief round
his throat, showed that he had not found leisure since
he left the court to make any alteration in his dress:
while the slovenly style of the remainder of his costume
warranted the inference that his personal appearance
would not have been very much improved if he had.
Books of practice, heaps of papers, and opened letters,
were scattered over the table, without any attempt at
order or arrangement; the furniture of the room was
old and ricketty; the doors of the bookcase were rotting
in their hinges; the dust flew out from the carpet in
little clouds at every step; the blinds were yellow with
age and dirt; the state of everything in the room showed,
with a clearness not to be mistaken, that Mr. Serjeant
Snubbin was far too much occupied with his professional
pursuits to take any great heed or regard of his personal
comforts."

It was a characteristic feature of the slowness of legal
process in those days that though the notice of action
was sent on August the 28th, 1827, the case was not ripe
for trial until February 14th of the next year—nearly
six months having elapsed. It is difficult to speculate as
to what this long delay was owing. There were only two
witnesses whose evidence had to be briefed—Mrs. Cluppins and Mrs. Sanders—and they were at hand. It is
odd, by the way, that they did not think of examining
little Tommy Bardell, the only one who actualiy witnessed the proceeding. True, he was of tender years—
about eight or ten—and the son of the Plaintiff, but
he must have " known the nature of an oath."

THE TRIAL.

At last the momentous morning came round. It was the fourteenth of February, Valentine's Day, 1828—one not of good omen for the Plaintiff.* The Defendant's party was rather gloomy at breakfast, when Perker, by way of encouraging his client, uttered some *dicta* as to the chances of the Jury having had a good breakfast. " Discontented or hungry jurymen, my dear Sir, always find for the Plaintiff." " Bless my heart," said Mr. Pickwick, looking very blank, " What do they do that for ! "

The party then got into hackney coaches and was driven to the Guildhall, where the case was to be tried at ten o'clock precisely.

How dramatic Boz has made the " calling of the Jury," which might be thought an uninteresting and prosaic operation enough. It was a special jury, which entailed one guinea per head extra expense on Mr. Pickwick. He had, of course, asked for it : but Dodson and Fogg would have been well content with and perhaps even have preferred a common jury. Now-a-days, special jurors, though summoned largely, have to be

* So confused is the chronology of *Pickwick*, that it is difficult to fix the exact date of the Trial. Boz, writing some ten years after the event, seems to have got a little confused and uncertain as to the exact year of the Trial. He first fixed the opening of the story in 1817 : but on coming to the compromising incident in Goswell Street, which occurred only a few weeks later, he changed the year to 1827. Then Jingle's anachronism of the French Revolution of July suggested that the new date would not do. So 1830 was next adopted. But this did not end the matter, for in the " errata " we are directed to change this date back again to 1827. And so it now stands. The Trial therefore really took place on April 1, 1828.

EXTERIOR OF THE GUILDHALL COURT.—NOW CITY MUSEUM.

INTERIOR OF THE GUILDHALL COURT, *circa* 1830.

(From an original drawing by T. Allen.)

almost coerced into attending. A fine of ten pounds is imposed, but this is almost invariably remitted on affidavit. The common jurors, moreover, do not show the reluctance to " serve " of Groffin, the chemist. A guinea is not to be despised. There are, as it were, *professional* common jurors who hang about the Courts in the hope of being thus called as " understudies." On this occasion what was called a *Tales* was prayed for, and two common jurors were pressed into the service : and " a greengrocer and a chemist were caught directly."

It is impossible to say too much of the completeness with which the legal scene is put forward. Everything is dealt with. We have perfect sketches of the judge, the ushers, the jury, the counsel on the case, the witnesses, the barristers, the attorneys; we have the speeches, the methods of examination and cross-examination.

There is nothing better or more life-like than the sketch of the court in the chill morning, and before the actors came on the scene—the inimitable description of the idle barristers hanging about " the Bar of England," which is accurate to this hour.

Few could describe effectively the peculiar appearance of a crowd of barristers assembled in a Court of Law. They are a type apart, and their odd head-gear accentuates all the peculiarities of their faces. No one has, however, succeeded so well as Boz in touching off their peculiarities. This sort of histrionic guise and bearing is assumed with a view to impose on his friends and the public, to suggest an idea that they have much or at least something to do.

" ' And that,' said Mr. Pickwick, pointing to a couple of enclosed seats on his right, ' that's where the jury-men sit, is it not ? '

' The identical place, my dear Sir,' replied Perker, tapping the lid of his snuff-box.

" Mr. Pickwick stood up in a state of great agitation, and took a glance at the court. There were already a pretty large sprinkling of spectators in the gallery, and a numerous muster of gentlemen in wigs in the barristers' seats, who presented, as a body, all that pleasing and extensive variety of nose and whisker for which the bar of England is so justly celebrated. Such of the gentlemen as had got a brief to carry, carried it in as conspicuous a manner as possible, and occasionally scratched their noses therewith, to impress the fact more strongly on the observation of the spectators." One of the happiest descriptions is surely that of the binding of law books. A law library is the most repulsive and uninteresting thing in the world. The colour of the leather is unhealthy and disagreeable, and the necessary shading is secured at the expense of grace. Boz characterises it as ' that under-done pie crust.' " Other gentlemen, who had no briefs to show, carried under their arms goodly octavos, with a red label behind, and that under-done-pie-crust-coloured cover, which is technically known as " law calf." Others, who had neither briefs nor books, thrust their hands into their pockets, and looked as wise as they conveniently could ; while others, again, moved here and there with great restlessness and earnestness of manner, content to awaken thereby the admiration and astonishment of the uninitiated stranger. The whole, to the great wonderment of Mr. Pickwick, were divided into little groups, who were chatting and discussing the news of the day in the most unfeeling manner possible—just as if no trial at all were coming on.

" A bow from Mr. Phunky, as he entered, and took his seat behind the row appropriated to the King's Counsel, attracted Mr. Pickwick's attention ; and he had scarcely returned it, when Mr. Serjeant Snubbin appeared, followed by Mr. Mallard, who half hid the Serjeant behind a large crimson bag, which he placed on his table, and after shaking hands with Perker, withdrew. Then there entered two or three more Serjeants, and among them, one with a fat body and a red face, who nodded in a friendly manner to Mr. Serjeant Snubbin, and said it was a fine morning.

'Who's that red-faced man, who said it was a fine morning and nodded to our counsel?' whispered Mr. Pickwick.

'Mr. Serjeant Buzfuz,' replied Perker. 'He's opposed to us; he leads on the other side. That gentleman behind him is Mr. Skimpin, his junior.'

"Mr. Pickwick was just on the point of inquiring, with great abhorrence of the man's cold-blooded villainy, how Mr. Serjeant Buzfuz, who was counsel for the opposite party, dared to presume to tell Mr. Serjeant Snubbin, who was counsel for him, that it was a fine morning,—when he was interrupted by a general rising of the barristers, and a loud cry of 'Silence!' from the officers of the court. Looking round, he found that this was caused by the entrance of the Judge."

On reaching the Court, Perker said, "put Mr. Pickwick's friends in the students' box. Mr. Pickwick had better sit by me." This useful provision for the instruction of legal probationers has fallen into desuetude —no place is reserved for the students now-a-days. Lord Campbell describes the custom and recalls an incident that occurred when he was sitting in the students' box, close to the Bench.

There were some matters of procedure which have since been changed—such as Mr. Skimpin "calling for" Winkle, and the latter answering. This is now done by an Officer of the Court. Skimpin also asks Winkle his name, as a first question, though he had been sworn and had given it. And the *mal-entendu* as to "Daniel Nathaniel" could not then have occurred, as the Officer would have obtained the name correctly. Another un-

D

usual thing was that Buzfuz, after his long and rather exhausting speech, should have examined the first witness. Now-a-days the junior would do this. We may note that at this time it was always "my Lord," and "your Lordship," with the full natural sound—we had not yet got to the clipped "M'lud," and "your Ludship." Perhaps this form *was* actually used by the Counsel but was not noticed by Boz, or seemed to him the right thing. The King's Counsel were behind and could stoop down to consult their solicitors.

This minute observation and particularity of Boz is further shown in his noting the very places where the Attorneys sat, and which he describes. They had the seats next the table :

" You are quite right," said Buzfuz later on, answering the whisper of Dodson and Fogg, after Sam's awkward revelation. How often have we seen these hasty communications, which are not without their dramatic effect.

THE JUDGE.

Mr. Pickwick, unfortunate in his Counsel, his Solicitor, his Jury—one of prejudiced tradesmen—was also to be unlucky in the Judge who tried his case. No doubt Perker had comforted him : "no matter how it goes, however unfair Buzfuz may be, we have a judge to hold the scales fair and keep the jury straight. The Lord Chief Justice of the Common Pleas, the Right Hon. Sir NICHOLAS CONYNGHAM TINDAL is a man of immense reputation at the Bar. We are most fortunate in having him." Judge then of the disappointment when on coming to court it was found that Sir Stephen Gaselee was to take the case " owing to the absence of the Chief Justice, occasioned by indisposition." (I protest that at times one does not know whether we are following out a course of real events, or tracing the incidents of a fiction, so wonderfully does Boz make his fiction blend with reality.) This was a serious blow. Tindal was an admirable judge. Did not his chroniclers write of him : " His sagacity, impartiality and plain sense, his industry and clear sightedness made him an admiration of non-professional spectators : while among lawyers he was very highly esteemed *for his invariable kindness to all who appeared before him.* He retained to the last their respect and affection." With such a man presiding Sergeant Buzfuz's eccentric violence and abuse of the defendant would have been restrained (" having the outward appearance of a man and not of a monster.") Mr. Skimpin's gross insinuations, to wit, that Winkle was "telegraphing" to his friend, would have been summarily put down, and all "bullying" checked; more, he would have calmly kept Counsel's attention to the issue. This perfect impartiality would have made him show to the Jury how little evidence there was to support the plaintiff's case. Instead came this unlucky indisposition: and his place was taken by "my Brother Gaselee:" with what results Mr. Pickwick was to learn disastrously.

It is curious, however, that the Chief Justice, in spite of his indisposition, should still be associated with the case; for he had tried the momentous case of Norton *v.* Melbourne, and had heard there letters read, which were parodied in the "chops and tomato sauce" correspondence, so Boz had him well before him. The case had to be tried at the Guildhall Sessions; so a fair and rational judge would have spoilt all sport. Further, as Boz had seen the fairness and dignity of the Chief Justice he was naturally reluctant to exhibit him unfavorably. The only thing was to make the Chief Justice become suddenly "indisposed," and have his place taken by a grotesque judge.

The Judge who was to try the case, Mr. Justice Stareleigh, as is well known, was drawn from Sir Stephen Gaselee, of whose name Stareleigh is a sort of synonym. Serjeant Gaselee was once well known in the prosecutions directed against Radicals and so-called Reformers, but *Pickwick* has given him a greater reputation. The baiting he received from patriotic advocates may have inflamed his temper and made him irritable. He is described by one author, in a most humorous, if personal fashion. He was "a most particularly short man, and so fat that he seemed all face and waistcoat. He rolled in upon two little turned legs, and having bobbed gravely to the bar who bobbed gravely to him, put his little legs under the table, when all you could see of

him was two queer little eyes, one broad, pink face, and
somewhere about half of a big and very comical-looking
wig." All through he is shown as arrogant and incapable, and also as making some absurd mistakes.

It will be a surprise to most people to learn that this
picture is no more than an amusing caricature, and that
the judge was really a person of high character, He is
described as "a very painstaking, upright judge, and,
in his private capacity, a worthy and benevolent man."
Thus, Mr. Croker, who, however, supplies a sound reason
for his being the subject of such satire. "With many
admirable qualities both of head and heart, he had
made himself a legitimate object of ridicule by his
explosions on the Bench." Under such conditions, the
Bar, the suitors and the public had neither the wish
nor the opportunity to search for extenuating excuses
in his private life. They suffered enough from the
"explosions" and that was all that concerned them.
He had been fourteen years on the Bench, and, like
Stareleigh, belonged to the Common Pleas. He was
suffering too from infirmities, particularly from deaf-
ness, and appears to have misapprehended statements
in the same grotesque fashion that he mistook Winkle's
name.

Boz's fashion of burlesque, by the way, is happily
shown in his treatment of this topic. Another would
have been content with "Daniel," the simple misappre-
hension. "Nathaniel, sir," says Winkle. "Daniel—
any other name?" "Nathaniel, sir—my lord, I mean."
"*Nathaniel Daniel—or Daniel Nathaniel?*" "No, my
lord, only Nathaniel, not Daniel at all."

"What did you tell me it was Daniel for, then, sir?"

"I didn't, my lord."

"You did, sir. *How could I have got Nathaniel in
my notes, unless you told me so, sir?*"

How admirable is this. The sly satire goes deeper, as

Judges, under less gross conditions, have often made this illogical appeal to " my notes."

Though not gifted with oratorical powers which were likely to gain him employment as a leader, Gaselee's reputation for legal knowledge soon recommended him to a judge's place. He was accordingly selected on July 1st, 1824, to fill a vacancy in the Court of Common Pleas. In that Court he sat for nearly fourteen years " with the character of a painstaking judge, and in his private capacity as a worthy and benevolent man." Thus Mr. Foss, F.S.A.

The reader will have noted the Judge's severity to poor Groffin, the chemist, who had pleaded the danger of his boy mistaking oxalic acid for Epsom salts. Could it be that the Judge's experience as the son of a provincial doctor, had shown what class of man was before him ? Later, unexpectedly, we learn that the Judge was a steady member for fourteen years of the Royal Humane Society, of which institution he was also a Vice-President.

But we now come to a most extraordinary thing— the result of the young author's telling and most sarcastic portrait of the irascible little judge. It is curious that Forster, while enumerating various instances of Boz's severe treatment of living persons, as a sort of chastisement for their defects of manner or character, seems not to have thought of this treatment of the judge—and passes it by. Nor did he notice the prompt result that followed on the sketch. The report of the trial appeared in the March number, 1837—and we are told, the luckless judge retired from the Bench, shortly after the end of Hilary Term, that is in April or the beginning of May. We may assume that the poor gentleman could not endure the jests of his *confrères* or the scarcely concealed tittering of the Barristers, all of whom had of course devoured and enjoyed the number.

We may say that the learned Sergeant Buzfuz was not likely to be affected in any way by *his* picture; it may indeed have added to his reputation. I confess to some sympathy for the poor old judge who was thus driven from the Bench. Sam Foote was much given to this sort of personal attack, and made the lives of some of his victims wretched. Boz, however, seems to have felt himself called upon to act thus as public executioner on two occasions only. After the fall of the judge in June, 1837, he wanted a model for a tyrannical magistrate in *Oliver Twist*—and Mr. Laing, the Hatton Garden Magistrate—a harsh, ferocious personage, at once occurred to him. He wrote accordingly to one of his friends that he wished to be *smuggled* into his office some morning to study him. This "smuggling" of course meant the placing him where he would not be observed—as a magistrate knowing his "sketches" might recognise him. "I know the man perfectly well" he added. So he did, for he forgot that he had introduced him already in *Pickwick* as Nupkins—whose talk is exactly alike, in places almost word for word to that of "Mr. Fang."

These palliations, Boz, a young fellow of three and twenty or so, did not pause to weigh. He only saw a testy, red-faced old fellow with goggle eyes, and seventy-four years old, and past his work. His infirmities already made him incapable of carrying through the business of the Court as the mistake, "Is it Daniel Nathaniel or Nathaniel Daniel?" shows. It is curious, however, that this weakness of misapprehending names is described of another judge, Arabin —a strange grotesque. Theodore Hook gives an amusing specimen in his Gilbert Gurney.

From the general description in the text, it is evident Stareleigh was the prey of gouty affections—which swelled him into grotesque shape, and he found him-

self unequal to the office. He died two years after his
retirement at No. 13, Montagu Place, Russell Square;
so that the Judge in Bardell *v.* Pickwick was living close
to Perker the Attorney in the same case. Here we seem
to mix up the fictional and the living characters, but
this is the law of *Pickwick*—the confines between the
two worlds being quite confused or broken down. The
late commander of our forces in China, Sir A. Gaselee,
is of this family. It should be remembered, however,
when we think of this judge's frowardness, that judge's
in those times were dictatorial and carried matters with
a high hand. There were often angry conflicts between
them, and members of the Bar, and Stareleigh was really
not so very tyrannical. He did what so many judges
do—took a side from the first, and had decided in his
own mind that Mr. Pickwick could not possibly have a
case. That curious form of address from the Bench
is now no longer heard—"who is with you, *Brother
Buzfuz?*" Judges and sergeants were then common
members of the Guild—both wore the "coif."

THE COURT.

When the swearing of the jury is going on, how good, and how natural is the scene with the unfortunate chemist.

"'Answer to your names, gentlemen that you may be sworn,' said the gentleman in black. 'Richard Up-witch.'

'Here,' said the greengrocer.

'Thomas Groffin.'

'Here,' said the chemist.

'Take the book, gentlemen. You shall well and truly try—'

'I beg this court's pardon,' said the chemist, who was a tall, thin, yellow-visaged man, 'but I hope this court will excuse my attendance.'

'On what grounds, sir?" replied Mr. Justice Stare-leigh.

'I have no assistant, my Lord,' said the chemist.

'I can't help that, sir,' replied Mr. Justice Stareleigh. 'You should hire one.'

'I can't afford it, my Lord,' rejoined the chemist.

'Then you ought to be able to afford it, sir,' said the judge, reddening; for Mr. Justice Stareleigh's temper bordered on the irritable, and brooked not contradiction.

'I know I *ought* to do, if I got on as well as I de-served, but I don't, my Lord,' answered the chemist.

'Swear the gentleman,' said the judge, peremptorily.

The officer had got no farther than the 'You shall

well and truly try,' when he was again interrupted by
the chemist.

'I am to be sworn, my Lord, am I?' said the chemist.

'Certainly, sir,' replied the testy little judge.

'Very well, my Lord,' replied the chemist in a re-
signed manner. 'There'll be murder before this trial's
over; that's all. Swear me, if you please, sir;' and
sworn the chemist was, before the judge could find words
to utter.

'I merely wanted to observe, my Lord,' said the
chemist, taking his seat with great deliberation, 'that
I've left nobody but an errand boy in my shop. He is
a very nice boy, my Lord, but he is not acquainted with
drugs; and I know that the prevailing impression on
his mind is, that Epsom salts means oxalic acid; and
syrup of senna, laudanum. That's all, my Lord.' With
this, the tall chemist composed himself into a comfort-
able attitude, and, assuming a pleasant expression of
countenance, appeared to have prepared himself for the
worst."

One who was born in the same year as Boz, but
who was to live for thirty years after him. Henry
Russell — composer and singer of "The Ivy Green"
—was, when a youth, apprenticed to a chemist, and
when about ten years old, that is five years before Bardell *v.* Pickwick, was left in charge of the shop. He
discovered just in time that he had served a customer
who had asked for Epsom salts with poison sufficient to
kill fifty people. On this he gave up the profession. I
have little doubt that he told this story to his friend a
dozen years later, and that it was on Boz's mind when
he wrote. Epsom salts was the drug mentioned in both
instances.

It must be said that even in our day a defendant for
Breach, with Mr. Pickwick's story and surroundings,
would have had small chance with a city jury. They

saw before them a benevolent-looking Lothario, of a Quaker-like air, while all the witnesses against him were his three most intimate friends and his own man.

We have, of course, testy judges now, who may be "short" in manner, but I think it can be affirmed that no judge of our day could behave to counsel or witnesses as Mr. Justice Stareleigh did. It is, in fact, now the tone for a judge to affect a sort of polished courtesy, and to impart a sort of light gaiety to the business he is transacting. All asperity and tyrannous rudeness is held to be out of place. Hectoring and bullying of witnesses will not be tolerated. The last exhibition was perhaps that of the late Dr. Kenealy in the Tichborne case.

All the swearing of jurymen before the court, with the intervention of the judge, has been got rid of. The Master of the Court, or Chief Clerk, has a number of interviews—at his public desk—with important individuals, bringing him signed papers. These are excuses of some sort—medical certificates, etc.—with a view to be "let off" serving. Some—most, perhaps—are accepted, some refused. A man of wealth and importance can have little difficulty. Of course this would be denied by the jurists: but, somehow, the great guns contrive not to attend. At ten o'clock this officer proceeds to swear the jury, which is happily accomplished by the time the judge enters.

SERJEANT BUZFUZ.

Mr. Pickwick, considering the critical nature of his case, was certainly unfortunate in his solicitor, as well as in the Counsel selected by his solicitors. The other side were particularly favoured in this matter. They had a pushful bustling "wide-awake" firm of solicitors, who let not a point escape. Sergeant Buzfuz was exactly the sort of advocate for the case—masterful, unscrupulous, eloquent, and with a singularly ingenious faculty

SERJEANT BUZFUZ, K.C.

for putting everything on his client's side in the best light, and his adversary's in the worst. He could "tear a witness to pieces," and turn him inside out. His junior, Skimpin, was glib, ready-armed at all points, and singularly adroit in "making a hare" of any wit-

ness who fell into his hands, *teste* Winkle. He had all
the professional devices for dealing with a witness's an-
swers, and twisting them to his purpose, at his fingers'
ends. He was the Wontner or Ballantyne of his day.
Mr. Pickwick's "bar" was quite outmatched. They
were rather a feeble lot, too respectable altogether, and
really not familiar with this line of business. Even the
judge was against them from the very start, so Mr.
Pickwick had very poor chances indeed. All this was
due to that old-fashioned and rather incapable "Family
Solicitor" Perker.

Serjeant Buzfuz is known the world all over, at least
wherever English is known. I myself was once startled
in a fashionable West End church to hear a preacher,
when emphasizing the value and necessity of Prayer,
and the certainty with which it is responded to, use
this illustration: "As Serjeant Buzfuz said to Sam
Weller, '*There is little to do and plenty to get.*'" Need-
less to say, an amused smile, if not a titter, passed
round the congregation. But it is the Barrister who
most appreciates the learned Serjeant. For the topics
he argued and his fashion of arguing them, bating a not
excessive exaggeration, comes home to them all. Nay,
they must have a secret admiration, and fondly think
how excellently well such and such topics are put, and
how they must have told with a jury.

Buzfuz, it is now well known, was drawn from a leading serjeant of his day, Serjeant Bompas, K.C. Not so
long since I was sitting by Bompas's son, the present
Judge Bompas, at dinner, and a most agreeable causeur
he was. Not only did Boz sketch the style and fashion
of the serjeant, but it is clear that Phiz drew the figure
and features.

"I am the youngest son of Serjeant Bompas," Judge
Bompas writes to me, "and have never heard it doubted
that the name Buzfuz was taken from my father who

was at that time considered a most successful advocate.
I think he may have been chosen for the successful
advocate because he was so successful : but I have never
been able to ascertain that there was any other special
resemblance.   I do not remember my father myself : he
died when I was eight years old.   But I am told I am
like him in face.   He was tall (five feet ten inches) and
a large man, very popular, and very excitable in his
cases, so that I am told that Counsel against him used
to urge him, out of friendship, not to get so agitated.
A connection of mine who knew him well, went over to
hear Charles Dickens read the Trial Scene, to see if he
at all imitated him in voice or manner, but told me
that he did not do so at all.   I think, therefore, that
having chosen his name, as a writer might now that of
Sir Charles Russell, he then drew a general type of
barrister, as he thought it might be satirised.   My
father, like myself, was on the Western Circuit and
leader of it at the time of his death."

"I had a curious episode happen to me once.   A
client wrote to apply to the court to excuse a juror on
the ground that he was a chemist and had no assistant
who understood the drugs.   It was not till I made the
application and the Court began to laugh that I remembered the Pickwick Trial.   I believe the application
was quite bonâ fide, and not at all an imitation of it."
An interesting communication from one who might be
styled "Buzfuz's son;" and, as Judge Bompas alludes
to his own likeness to his sire, I may add that the likeness to the portrait in the court scene, is very striking
indeed.   There is the same fullness of face, the large
features.   Busfuz was certainly a counsel of power and
ability, and I think lawyers will admit he managed
Mrs. Bardell's case with much adroitness.   His speech,
besides being a sort of satirical abstract of the un-
amiable thundering boisterousness addressed to juries

in such cases, is one of much ability. He makes the most
of every topic that he thought likely to "tell" on a
city jury. We laugh heartily at his would-be solemn
and pathetic passages, but these are little exaggerated.
Buzfuz's statement is meant to show how counsel, quite
legitimately, can bring quite innocent acts to the support of their case by marshalling them in suspicious
order, and suggesting that they had a connection with
the charge made. Many a client thus becomes as be-
wildered as Mr. Pickwick was, on seeing his own harmless proceedings assuming quite a guilty complexion.

Serjeant Buzfuz-Bompas died at the age of fifty-three,
at his house in Park Road, Regents Park, on February
29th, 1844. He was then, comparatively, a young man,
and must have had ability to have attained his position
so early. He was called to the Bar in 1815, and began
as Serjeant in 1827, in Trinity Term, only a year or so
before the famous case was tried.

So dramatic is the whole "Trial" in its action and
characters, that it is almost fit for the stage as it stands.
There have been a great number of versions, one by the
author's son, Charles "the Younger," one by Mr. Hol-
lingshead, and so on. It is a favorite piece for charitable
benefits, and a number of well-known performers often
volunteer to figure as "Gentlemen of the Jury." Buzfuz
has been often played by Mr. Toole, but his too farcical
methods scarcely enhanced the part. The easiness of
comedy is essential. That sound player Mr. James
Fernander is the best Buzfuz that I have seen.

There is a French translation of *Pickwick*, in which
the general spirit of the "Trial" is happily conveyed.
Thus Mr. Phunky's name is given as "M. Finge," which
the little judge mistakes for "M. Singe." Buzfuz's
speech too is excellent, especially his denouncing the
Defendant's coming with his chops "*et son ignoble bas-
sinoire*," i.e., warming pan.

THE OPENING SPEECH.

Buzfuz's great speech is one of the happiest parodies
in the language. Never was the forensic jargon and
treatment so humorously set forth—and this because of
the perfect *sincerity* and earnestness with which it was
done. There is none of the far-fetched, impossible
exaggeration—the form of burlesque which Theodore
Hook or Albert Smith might have attempted. It is, in
fact, a real speech, which might have been delivered to
a dull-headed audience without much impairing credi-
bility. Apart from this it is a most effective harangue
and most plausible statement of the Plaintiff's case.

A little professional touch, which is highly significant
as part of the pantomine, and which Boz made very
effective at the reading, was the Serjeant's dramatic pre-
paration for his speech. "Having whispered to Dodson
and conferred briefly with Fogg, *he pulled his gown over
his shoulders, settled his wig*, and addressed the Jury."
Who has not seen this bit of business?

Again, Juries may have noted that the Junior as he
rises to speak, mumbles something that is quite inaudible,
and which nobody attends to. This is known as "opening the pleadings."

"The ushers again called silence, and Mr. Skimpin
proceeded to 'open the case;' and the case appeared to
have very little inside it when he had opened it, for he
kept such particulars as he knew, completely to himself,
and sat down, after a lapse of three minutes, leaving the
jury in precisely the same advanced stage of wisdom as
they were in before.

Serjeant Buzfuz then rose with all the majesty and
dignity which the grave nature of the proceedings de-
manded, and having whispered to Dodson, and conferred briefly with Fogg, pulled his gown over his
shoulders, settled his wig, and addressed the jury."

A most delightful legal platitude, as one might call
it, is to be found in the opening of the learned Sergeant's speech. It is a familiar, transparent thing,
often used to impose on the Jury. As Boz says of
another topic, "Counsel often begins in this way because it makes the jury think what sharp fellows they
must be." "You have heard from my learned friend,
gentlemen," continued the Serjeant, well knowing that
from the learned friend alluded to they had heard just
nothing at all, "you have heard from my learned friend,
that this is an action for Breach of Promise of Marriage,
in which the damages are laid at £1,500. But you have
*not heard from my learned friend, inasmuch as it did not
lie within my learned friend's province to tell you*, what
are the facts and circumstances of the case." This rich
bit of circumlocution is simple nonsense, in rotund
phrase, and meant to suggest the imposing majesty
of legal process. The Jury knew perfectly beforehand
what they were going to try : but were to be impressed
by the magnifying agency of legal processes, and would
be awe stricken accordingly. The passage, "inasmuch
as it did not lie within my learned friend's province to
tell you," is a delightful bit of cant. In short, the
Jury was thus admitted to the secret legal arena, and
into community with the learned friends themselves,
and were persuaded that they were very sharp fellows
indeed. What pleasant satire is here, on the mellifluous
"openings" of Counsel, the putting a romantic gloss on
the most prosaic incidents.

A sucking Barrister might well study this speech of
Buzfuz as a guide to the conducting of a case, and above

E

all of rather a "shaky" one. Not less excellent is his smooth and plausible account of Mrs. Bardell's setting up in lodging letting. He really makes it "interesting." One thinks of some fluttering, helpless young widow, setting out in the battle of life.

He describes the poor innocent lady putting a bill in her window, "and let me entreat the attention of the Jury to the wording of this document—'Apartments furnished for a single gentleman!' Mrs. Bardell's opinions of the opposite sex, gentlemen, were derived from a long contemplation of the inestimable qualities of her lost husband. She had no fear—she had no distrust—she had no suspicion—all was confidence and reliance. 'Mr. Bardell,' said the widow: 'Mr. Bardell was a man of honour—Mr. Bardell was a man of his word—Mr. Bardell was no deceiver—Mr. Bardell was once a single gentleman himself; to single gentlemen I look for protection, for assistance, for comfort, and for consolation—in single gentlemen I shall perpetually see something to remind me of what Mr. Bardell was, when he first won my young and untried affections; to a single gentleman, then, shall my lodgings be let. Actuated by this beautiful and touching impulse (among the best impulses of our imperfect nature, gentlemen), the lonely and desolate widow dried her tears, furnished her first floor, caught her innocent boy to her maternal bosom, and put the bill up in her parlour window. Did it remain there long? No. The serpent was on the watch, the train was laid, the mine was preparing, the sapper and miner was at work. Before the bill had been in the parlour window three days—three days, gentlemen— a being, erect upon two legs, and bearing all the outward semblance of a man, and not of a monster, knocked at the door of Mrs. Bardell's house. He enquired within.

Those who attended the Reading will recall the ad-

mirable briskness, and more admirable spirit with which
Boz delivered the passage "by the evidence of the
unimpeachable female whom I shall place in that "—here
he brought down his palm with a mighty slap on the
desk, and added, after a moment's pause, " *Box* before
you." It was that *preceding* of the stroke that told.
So real was it, one fancied oneself listening to some
obstreperous counsel. In all true acting—notably on
the French boards—the gesture should a little precede
the utterance. So the serjeant knew something of art.

When Mr. Pickwick gave an indignant start on hearing himself described as a heartless villain how cleverly
does the capable Buzfuz turn the incident to profit.

" 'I say systematic villany, gentlemen,' said Serjeant

MR. PICKWICK AS A MONSTER.

Buzfuz, looking through Mr. Pickwick, and talking *at*
him; 'and when I say systematic villiany, let me tell
the defendant, Pickwick, if he be in court, as I am in-

formed he is, that it would have been more decent in
him, more becoming, in better judgment and in better
taste, if he had stopped away. Let me tell him, gentlemen, that any gestures of dissent or disapprobation in
which he may indulge in this court will not go down
with you; that you will know how to value, and to
appreciate them; and let me tell him further, as my
lord will tell you, gentlemen, that a counsel, in the
discharge of his duty to his client, is neither to be
intimidated nor bullied, nor put down; and that any
attempt to do either the one or the other, or the first
or the last, will recoil on the head of the attempter, be
he plaintiff or be he defendant, be his name Pickwick, or
Noakes, or Stoakes, or Stiles, or Brown, or Thompson.'
This little divergence from the subject in hand, had
of course the intended effect of turning all eyes to Mr.
Pickwick."

We relish, too, another "common form." When the
Serjeant found that his jest as to "greasing the wheels
of Mr. Pickwick's slow-coach" had somewhat missed
fire—a thing that often unaccountably happens, in the
case of the "twelve intelligent men," the Serjeant knew
how to adroitly recover himself.

"He paused in this place to see whether the jury
smiled at his joke; but as nobody took it but the greengrocer, whose sensitiveness on the subject was very
probably occasioned by his having subjected a chaise-
cart to the process in question on that identical morning, the learned serjeant considered it advisable to
undergo a slight relapse into the dismals before he concluded.

'But enough of this, gentlemen,' said Mr. Serjeant
Buzfuz, 'it is difficult to smile with an aching heart; it
is ill jesting when our deepest sympathies are awakened.
My client's hopes and prospects are ruined, and it is no
figure of speech to say that her occupation is gone

indeed. The bill is down—but there is no tenant. Eligible single gentlemen pass and repass—but there is no invitation for them to enquire within or without. All is gloom and silence in the house; even the voice of the child is hushed; his infant sports are disregarded when his mother weeps; his " alley tors " and his " commoneys " are alike neglected; he forgets the long familiar cry of " knuckle down," and at tip-cheese, or odd and even, his hand is out. But Pickwick, gentlemen, Pickwick, the ruthless destroyer of this domestic oasis in the desert of Goswell Street—Pickwick, who has choked up the well, and thrown ashes on the sward—Pickwick, who comes before you to-day with his heartless tomato sauce and warming-pans—Pickwick still rears his head with unblushing effrontery, and gazes without a sigh on the ruin he has made. Damages, gentlemen—heavy damages is the only punishment with which you can visit him.' "

THE INCRIMINATING LETTERS.

"I shall prove to you, gentlemen, that *about a year ago Pickwick suddenly began to absent himself from home,* during long intervals, ('on Pickwick Tours,') *as if with the intention of breaking off from my client :* but I shall show you also that his resolutions were not at that time sufficiently strong, or that his better feelings conquered, *if better feelings he has :* or that the charms and accomplishments of my client prevailed against his unmanly intentions." We may note the reserve which suggested a struggle going on in Mr. Pickwick. And how persuasive is Buzfuz's *exegesis !* Then, on the letters :

"These letters bespeak the character of the man. They are not open, fervid, eloquent epistles breathing nothing but the language of affectionate attachment. They are *covert, sly,* under-hand communications, but, fortunately, far more conclusive than if couched in the most glowing language. *Letters that must be viewed with a cautious and suipicious eye : letters that were evidently intended at the time, by Pickwick, to mislead and delude any third parties into whose hands they might fall."* The gravity and persuasiveness of all this is really *impayable.* "Let me read the first : 'Garraway's, twelve o'clock. Dear Mrs. B., Chops and tomato sauce. Yours, Pickwick.' Gentlemen, what does this mean ? Chops and tomato sauce. Yours, Pickwick. Chops ! Gracious Heavens !—and tomato sauce ! Gentlemen, is the happiness of a sensitive and confiding female *to be trifled* away by such artifices as these ? *The next has no date whatever which is in itself suspicious :* ' Dear Mrs. B., I shall not be at home uutil to-morrow. Slow coach.' And then follows the very remarkable expression, ' Don't trouble yourself about the warming pan.' "

There is a little bit of serious history connected with these letters which I was the first I think to discover. They were intended to satirise the trivial scraps brought forward in Mrs. Norton's matrimonial case—Norton *v.* Lord Melbourne. My late friend, " Charles Dickens the younger," as he used to call himself, in his notes on *Pickwick,* puts aside this theory altogether as a mere unfounded fancy ; but it will be seen there cannot be a doubt in the matter. Sir W. Follett laid just as much stress on these scraps as Serjeant Buzfuz did on his : he even used the phrase, " it seems there may be latent love like latent heat, in these productions." We have also, " Yours Melbourne," like " Yours Pickwick," the latter signing as though he were a Peer. " There is another of these notes," went on Sir William, " How are you ? " " Again there is no beginning you see." " The next has no date, which is in itself suspicious," Buzfuz would have added. Another ran—" I will call about half past four, Yours." " *These* are the only notes that have been found," added the counsel, with due gravity, " *they seem to import much more than mere words convey.*" After this can there be a doubt ?

This case was tried in June, 1836, and, it must be borne in mind, caused a prodigious sensation all over the Kingdom. The Pickwick part, containing the description, appeared about December, six months afterwards. Only old people may recall Norton *v.* Melbourne, the fair Caroline's wrongs have long been forgotten ; but it is curious that the memory of it should have been kept alive in some sort by this farcical parody. Equally curious is it that the public should always have insisted that she was the heroine of yet another story, George

Meredith's *Diana*, though the author has disclaimed it over and over again.

The Serjeant's dealing with the warming pan topic is a truly admirable satiric touch, and not one bit far-fetched or exaggerated. Any one familiar with suspicious actions has again and again heard comments as plausible and as forced. " Don't trouble yourself about the warming pan! The warming pan! Why, gentlemen, who *does* trouble himself about a warming pen ?" A delicions *non sequitur*, sheer nonsense, and yet with an air of conviction that is irresistable. " When was the peace of mind of man or woman broken or disturbed by a warming pan which is in itself a harmless, a useful *and I will add, gentlemen*, a comforting article of domestic furniture ? " He then goes on ingeniously to suggest that it may be " a cover for hidden fire, a mere substitute for some endearing word or promise, *agreeably to a preconcerted system* of correspondence, artfully contrived by Pickwick *with a view* to his contemplated desertion and which I am not in a position to explain ? " Admirable indeed! One could imagine a city jury in their wisdom thinking that there must be *something* in this warming pan !

Not less amusing and plausible is his dealing with the famous topic of the " chops and tomato sauce," not " tomata " as Boz has it. I suppose there is no popular allusion better understood than this. The very man in the street knows all about it and what it means. Absurd as it may seem, it is hardly an exaggeration. Counsel every day give weight to points just as trivial and expound them elaborately to the jury. The Serjeant's burst of horror is admirable, " Gentlemen, *what does this mean ?* 'Chops and tomata sauce ! Yours Pickwick !' Chops! Gracious Heavens! What does this mean? Is the happiness of a sensitive and confiding female to be trifled away *by such shallcw artifices as these ?* "

I recall that admirable judge and pleasant man, the late Lord FitzGerald, who was fond of talking of this trial, saying to me that Buzfuz lost a good point here, as he might have dwelt on the mystic meaning of tomato which is the "love apple," that here was the "secret correspondence," the real "cover for hidden fire."

He concluded by demanding exemplary damages as "the recompense you can award my client. And for these damages she now appeals to an enlightened, a high-minded, a right feeling, a conscientious, a dispassionate, a sympathising, a contemplative jury of her civilized countrymen!"

THE PLAINTIFF'S CASE.

It was really of a very flimsy kind but "bolstered-up" and carried through by the bluster of the serjeant and the smartness of his junior. It rested first on a dialogue between Mr. Pickwick and his landlady which was overheard, in fact by several persons; second, on a striking situation witnessed by his three friends who entered unexectedly and surprised him with Mrs. Bardell in his arms; third, on some documentary evidence, and lastly, on a damaging incident disclosed by Winkle.

The first witness "put in the box," was Mrs. Martha Cluppins—an intimate friend of the plaintiffs.

We know that she was sister to Mrs. Raddle, who lived far away in Southwark, and was the landlady of Mr. Sawyer. She might have been cross-exmined with effect as to her story that she had been "out buying kidney pertaties," etc. Why buy these articles in Goswell Street and come all the way from Southwark? What was she doing there at all? This question could have been answered only in one way—which was that the genial author fancied at the moment she was living near Mrs. Bardell.

Besides this, there was another point which Snubbin, in cross-examination, ought to have driven home. Mrs. Cluppins was of an inferior type, of the common washer-woman or "charing" sort; her language was of Mrs. Gamp's kind; "which her name was" so and so. Yet, this creature, in another room, or on the stairs, the door being "on the jar," can repeat with her limited

appreciation, those dubious and imperfect utterances of
Mr. Pickwick! How could she remember all? Or could
she understand them? Impossible! She, however, may
have caught up something.

Winkle, too, said he heard something as he came up the
stairs—" Compose yourself my dear creature, for consider
if any one were to come," etc. But what could be the
value of evidence heard in this way? Would a jury
believe it? "Not only," as Sam said, "is 'wision limited,'"
but hearing also.

In short, the delicate subtleties of the conversation
between Mr. Pickwick and Mrs. Bardell would be wholly
lost in her hands. Persons of her class know nothing of
suggestion or double meanings or reserved intention,
everything for them must be in black and white. How
unlikely, therefore, that through the panels of a door or
through the half opened door, ("she said on the jar,")
could she catch the phrases and their meanings, and,
above all, retain them in her memory? No doubt, as the
counsel put it bluntly, she listened, and with all her ears.

However this may be, here is what Mrs. Cluppins
deposed to:

"'Mrs. Cluppins,' said Serjeant Buzfuz, 'pray compose yoursel, ma'am;' and, of course, directly Mrs.
Cluppins was desired to compose herself she sobbed with
increased violence, and gave divers alarming manifestations of an approaching fainting fit, or, as she afterwards
said, of her feelings being too many for her.

'Do you recollect, Mrs. Cluppins? said Serjeant Buzfuz, after a few unimportant questions—'do you recollect
being in Mrs. Bardell's back one pair of stairs, on one
particular morning in July last, when she was dusting
Mr. Pickwick's apartment?

' Yes, my Lord and jury, I do," replied Mrs. Cluppins.

'Mr. Pickwick's sitting-room was the first floor front,
I believe?

' Yes it were, sir,' replied Mrs. Cluppins.

'What were you doing in the back room, ma'am ? ' inquired the little judge.

' My Lord and jury,' said Mrs. Cluppins, with interesting agitation, 'I will not deceive you.'

' You had better not, ma'am,' said the little judge.'

'I was there,' resumed Mrs. Cluppins, 'unbeknown to Mrs. Bardell ; I had been out with a little basket, gentlemen, to buy three pounds of red kidney pertaties, which was three pound, tuppense ha'penny, when I see Mrs. Bardell's street door on the jar.'

' On the what ? ' exclaimed the little judge.

' Partly open, my Lord,' said Serjeant Snubbin.

' She *said* on the jar,' said the little judge with a cunning look.

' It's all the same, my lord,' said Serjeant Snubbin. The little judge looked doubtful, and said he'd make a note of it. Mrs. Cluppins then resumed—

'I walked in, gentlemen, just to say good mornin', and went in a permiscuous manner up-stairs, and into the back room. Gentlemen, there was the sound of voices in the front room, and—'

' And you listened, I believe, Mrs. Cluppins,' said Serjeant Buzfuz.

' Beggin' your pardon, sir,' replied Mrs. Cluppins, in a majestic manner, 'I would scorn the haction. The voices was very loud, sir, and forced themselves upon my ear.'

'Well, Mrs. Cluppins, you were not listening, but you heard the voices. Was one of those voices Mr. Pickwick's ? '

' Yes, it were, sir.' "

And Mrs. Cluppins, after distinctly stating that Mr. Pickwick addressed himself to Mrs. Bardell, repeated by slow degrees, and by dint of many questions the conversation with which our readers are already aquainted."

Now we have to turn back to one of the earlier passages in the story for the conversation between the pair, " with which the reader is already acquainted." Thus we shall know what Mrs. Cluppin's might have heard.

" Mr. Pickwick paced the room to and fro with hurried steps, popped his head out of the window at intervals of about three minutes each, constantly referred to his watch, and exhibited many other manifestations of impatience, very unusual with him. It was evident that something of great importance was in contemplation, but what that something was not even Mrs. Bardell herself had been enabled to discover.

'Mrs. Bardell,' said Mr. Pickwick at last, as that amiable female approached the termination of a prolonged dusting of the apartment.

' Sir,' said Mrs. Bardell.

' Your little boy is a very long time gone.'

' Why, it's a good long way to the Borough, sir,' remonstrated Mrs. Bardell.

' Ah,' said Pickwick, ' very true; so it is.'

Mr. Pickwick relapsed into silence, and Mrs. Bardell resumed her dusting.

'Mrs. Bardell,' said Mr. Pickwick, at the expiration of a few minutes.

' Sir,' said Mrs. Bardell again.

' Do you think it's a much greater expense to keep two people, than to keep one?'

' La, Mr. Pickwick,' said Mrs. Bardell, colouring up to the very border of her cap, as she fancied she observed a species of matrimonial twinkle in the eyes of her lodger, ' La, Mr. Pickwick, what a question!'

' Well, but *do* you?' inquired Mr. Pickwick.

'That depends—" said Mrs. Bardell, approaching the duster very near to Mr. Pickwick's elbow, which was planted on the table; ' that depends a good deal upon

the person, you know, Mr. Pickwick ; and whether it's
a saving and careful person, sir.'

'That's very true,' said Mr. Pickwick, 'but the person I have in my eye (here he looked very hard at Mrs.
Bardell) I think possesses these qualities ; and has,
moreover, a considerable knowledge of the world, and
a great deal of sharpness, Mrs. Bardell ; which may be
of .naterial use to me.'

'La, Mr. Pickwick,' said Mrs. Bardell ; the crimson
rising to her cap-border again.

'I do,' said Mr. Pickwick, growing energetic, as was
his wont in speaking of a subject which interested him,
'I do, indeed ; and to tell you the truth, Mrs. Bardell,
I have made up my mind.'

'Dear me, sir,' exclaimed Mrs. Bardell.

'You'll think it very strange, now,' said the amiable
Mr. Pickwick, with a good humoured glance at his
companion, 'that I never consulted you about this
matter, and never even mentioned it, till I sent your
little boy out this morning, eh ? '

Mrs. Bardell could only reply by a look. She had
long worshipped Mr. Pickwick at a distance, but here
she was, all at once, raised to a pinnacle to which her
wildest and most extravagant hopes and never dared to
aspire. Mr. Pickwick was going to propose—a delibe-
rate plan, too—sent her little boy to the Borough, to
get him out of the way—how thoughtful—how con-
siderate ! '

'Well,' said Mr. Pickwick, 'what do you think ? '

'Oh, Mr. Pickwick,' said Mrs. Bardell, trembling with
agitation, 'you're very kind, sir.'

'It'll save you a good deal of trouble, won't it ? ' said
Mr. Pickwick.

'Oh, I never thought anything of the trouble, sir,'
replied Mrs. Bardell ; 'and, of course, I should take
more trouble to please you then, than ever ; but it is so

kind of you, Mr. Pickwick, to have so much consideration for my loneliness.'

' Ah, to be sure,' said Mr. Pickwick : I never thought
of that. When I am in town, you'll always have somebody to sit with you. To be sure, so you will.'

'I'm sure I ought to be a very happy woman,' said
Mrs. Bardell.

' And your little boy—' said Mr. Pickwick.

'Bless his heart,' interposed Mrs. Bardell, with a
maternal sob.

' He, too, will have a companion,' resumed Mr. Pickwick, ' a lively one, who'll teach him, I'll be bound, more
tricks in a week than he would ever learn in a year.'
And Mr. Pickwick smiled placidly.

' Oh, you dear—' said Mrs. Bardell.

Mr. Pickwick started.

' Oh, you kind, good, playful dear,' said Mrs. Bardell ;
and without more ado, she rose from her chair, and flung
her arms round Mr. Pickwick's neck, with a cataract of
tears, and a chorus of sobs.

'Bless my soul,' cried the astonished Mr. Pickwick ;
—' Mrs. Bardell, my good woman—dear me, what a
situation—pray—consider, Mrs. Bardell, if anybody
should come.'

' O, let them come,' exclaimed Mrs. Bardell, fran-
tically.

' I'll never leave you, dear, kind, good soul.' And
with these words Mrs. Bardell clung the tighter."

Every utterance of the little Judge is in character,
from his first directions " go on." His suspicious question, " what were you doing in the back room, ma'am ? "
—and on Serjeant Buzfuz's sudden pause for breath,
when " the *silence* awoke Mr. Justice Stareleigh, who im-
mediateley wrote down something, with a pen without
any ink in it, and looked unusually profound, to impress
his jury with the belief that he always thought most

deeply with his eyes shut." Also when at the "on the jar" incident—he "looked doubtful, but said he'd make a note of it." So when Sam made one of his free and easy speeches, the Judge looked sternly at Sam for fully two minutes, but Sam's features were so perfectly calm that he said nothing. When Sam, too, made his witty *reposte* to Buzfuz as to his "wision being limited," we are told that there was a great laugh—that even "the little Judge smiled:" a good touch, for he enjoyed, like other judges, seeing his learned brother get a fall—'tis human nature.

It must be said the impression of a listener, who had heard all this could have been anything but favourable to Mr. Pickwick. No doubt there was his paternally benevolent character to correct it: but even this might go against him as it would suggest a sort of hypocrisy. Even the firmest friends, in their surprise, do not pause to debate or reason; they are astonished and wonder exceedingly.

WINKLE'S EVIDENCE.

Skimpin may have been intended for Wilkin, a later
Serjeant and well-known in the 'fifties, and whose style
and manner is reproduced. We could not ask a better
junior in a "touch and go" case. He was as ready to
take advantage of any opening as was the late Lord
Bowen, when he was junior in the Tichborne case.

MR. SKIMPIN.

On entering the Box, Mr. Winkle "bowed to the
Judge," with considerable deference, a politeness quite
thrown away. "Don't look at me sir," said the Judge
sharply, "look at the Jury." This was ungracious, but
judges generally don't relish any advances from witnesses or others.

When poor Winkle was accused by the Judge of
giving his name as Daniel, he was told that "he had
better be careful:" on which the ready Skimpin: "Now,
Mr. Winkle attend to me if you please: and let me

F

recommend you, for your own sake, to bear in mind his lordship's injunction to be careful." Thus by the agency of Judge and counsel witness was discredited at starting and of course flurried.

" ' I believe you are a particular friend of Pickwick, the defendant, are you not?'"

Winkle, eager to retrieve himself by being " careful " began—

' I have known Mr. Pickwick now as well as I recollect at this moment, nearly—'

' Pray, Mr. Winkle, don't evade the question. Are you, or are you not a particular friend of the defendant ? '

' I was just about to say that—'

' Will you, or will you not answer my question, sir ? '

' If you don't you'll be committed, sir,' interposed the little Judge.

' Come, sir,' said Mr. Skimpin, ' *yes or no, if you please.*'

' Yes, I am,' replied Mr. Winkle.

' *Yes, you are. And why couldn't you say that at once, sir ?* ' "

I think there is no more happy touch of legal satire in the books than that about " What the soldier said." It is perfect, so complete, that it is always understood by unprofessional readers. The lawyer feels at once that it is as true as it is happy.

" ' Little to do and plenty to get," said Serjeant Buzfuz to Sam.

" O, quite enough to get, sir, as the soldier said ven they ordered him three hundred and fifty lashes."

' *You must not tell us what the soldier or any other man said, sir ; it's not evidence,*' interposed the Judge.

Who will forget the roar that always greeted this sally when Boz read it, or the low and slow solemnity which he imparted to the Judge's dictum. As an illustration it is simply admirable.

Boz himself would have been pleased to find himself quoted in two impressive legal tomes of some 1800 pages. The great and laborious John Pitt Taylor could not have been wholly a legal dry-as-dust: for the man who could have gravely entered Bardell *v.* Pickwick in his notes and have quoted a passage must have had a share of humour.

Most people know that it is a strict principle that " hearsay evidence " of an utterance will not be accepted in lieu of that of the person to whom the remark was made. Neither can we think it out of probability that such an objection may have been made by some over punctilious judge wishing to restrain Sam's exuberance. A Scotch judge once quoted in court a passage from *The Antiquary* in which he said the true view of an intricate point was given ; but then Scott was a lawyer.

It is requisite, says Mr. John Pitt Taylor (p. 500) speaking of " hearsay evidence " that whatever facts a witness speaks, he should be confined to those lying within his own knowledge. For every witness should give his testimony on oath, and should be subject to cross examination. But testimony from the relation of third persons cannot be subject to these tests. This rule of exclusion has been recognised as a fundamental principle of the law of evidence ever since the time of Charles II. To this he adds a note, with all due gravity : " The rule excluding heresay evidence, or rather the mode in which that rule is frequently misunderstood in Courts of Justice, is amusingly caricatured by Mr. Dickens *in his report* of the case of Bardell *v.* Pickwick, p. 367."

Bardell *v.* Pickwick ! He thus puts it with the many thousand or tens of thousand cases quoted, and he has even found a place for it in his index of places. He then goes on to quote the passage, just as he would quote from Barnwall and Adolphus.

How sagacious—full of legal point—is Boz's comment on Winkle's incoherent evidence. Phunky asked him whether he had any reason to suppose that Pickwick was about to be married. "'Oh no; certainly not,' replied Mr. Winkle with so much eagerness, that Mr. Phunky ought to have got him out of the box with all possible dispatch. Lawyers hold out that there are two kinds of particularly bad witnesses: a reluctant witness, and a too willing witness;" and most true it is. Both commit themselves in each case, but in different ways. The matter of the former, and the manner of the latter do the mischief. The ideal witness affects indifference, and is as impartial as the record of a phonograph. It is wonderful where Boz learned all this. No doubt from his friend Talfourd, K.C., who carefully revised "The Trial."

Skimpin's interpretation of Mr. Pickwick's consolatory phrase, which he evidently devised on the spur of the moment, shows him to be a very ready, smart fellow.

"'Now, Mr. Winkle, I have only one more question to ask you, and I beg you to bear in mind his Lordship's caution. Will you undertake to swear that Pickwick, the Defendant, did not say on the occasion in question—"My dear Mrs. Bardell, you're a good creature; compose yourself to this situation, for to this situation you must come," or words to that effect?'

'I—I didn't understand him so, certainly,' said Mr. Winkle, astounded at this ingenious dove-tailing of the few words he had heard. 'I was on the staircase, and couldn't hear distinctly; the impression on my mind is—'

'The gentlemen of the jury want none of the impressions on your mind, Mr. Winkle, which I fear would be of little service to honest, straightforward men,' interposed Mr. Skimpin. 'You were on the staircase, and didn't distinctly hear; but you will swear that Pickwick

did not make use of the expressions I have quoted? Do
I understand that?'

'No, I will not,' replied Mr. Winkle; and down sat
Mr. Skimpin, with a triumphant countenance.

This "Will you swear he did *not*," etc., is a device
familiar to cross examiners, and is used when the witness
cannot be got to accept the words or admit that they
were used. It of course means little or nothing: but
its effect on the jury is that they come to fancy that
the words *may* have been used, and that the witness is
not very clear as to his recollection.

How well described, too, and satirised, is yet another
"common form" of the cross examiner, to wit the
"How often, Sir?" question. Winkle, when asked as
to his knowledge of Mrs. Bardell, replied that "he did
not know her, but that he had seen her." (I recall
making this very answer to Boz when we were both
driving through Sackville Street, Dublin. He had asked
"Did I know so-and-so?" when I promptly replied,
"I don't know him, but I have seen him." This rather
arrided him, as Elia would say.)

Skimpin went on: "'Oh, you don't know her, but you
have seen her.'

'Now have the goodness to tell the gentlemen of
the jury what you mean by *that*, Mr. Winkle.'

'I mean that I am not intimate with her, but that I
have seen her when I went to call on Mr. Pickwick, in
Goswell Street.'

'How often have you seen her, Sir?'

'How often?'

'*Yes, Mr. Winkle, how often?* I'll repeat the question
for you a dozen times, if you require it, Sir.' And the
learned gentlemen, with a firm and steady frown, placed
his hands on his hips, and smiled suspiciously to the jury.

"*On this question there arose the edifying brow-beating,
customary on such points.* First of all, Mr. Winkle said

it was quite impossible for him to say how many times he had seen Mrs. Bardell. Then he was asked if he had seen her twenty times, to which he replied, ' Certainly,— more than that.' And then he was asked whether he hadn't seen her a hundred times—whether he couldn't swear that he had seen her more than fifty times— whether he didn't know that he had seen her at least seventy-five times, and so forth ; the satisfactory con- clusion which was arrived at, at last, being—that he had better take care of himself, and mind what he was about. The witness having been, by these means, re- duced to the requisite ebb of nervous perplexity, the examination was concluded."

How excellent is this. Who has not heard the pro- cess repeated over and over again from the young fledgeling Counsel to the old " hardbitten " and ex- perienced K.C. ?

A young legal tyro might find profit as well as enter- tainment in carefully studying others of Mr. Skimpin's adroit methods in cross examination. They are in a manner typical of those in favour with the more ex- perienced members of the profession, allowing, of course, for a little humorous exaggeration. He will note also that Boz shows clearly how effective was the result of the processes. Here are a few useful recipes.

How to make a witness appear as though he wished to withhold the truth. How to highly discredit a witness by an opening question. How to insinuate inaccuracy. How to suggest that the witness is evading. How to deal with a statement of a particular number of instances. How to take advantage of a witness' glances. How to suggest another imputed meaning to a witness' statement and confuse him into accepting it.

Another happy and familiar form is Skimpin's inter- rogation of Winkle as to his " friends "—

" Are they here ? "

"Yes they are," said Mr. Winkle, *looking very earnestly towards the spot where his friends were stationed.*

As every one attending courts knows, this is an almost intuitive movement in a witness; he thinks it corroborates him somehow.

But how good Skimpin and how ready—

"'Pray attend to me, Mr. Winkle, and *never mind your friends,*' with another expressive look at the jury; '*they must tell their stories without any previous consultation with you,* if none has yet taken place,' another expressive look. 'Now Sir, tell what you saw, etc. '*Come, out with it, sir, we must* have it sooner or later.' The assumption here that the witness would keep back what he knew is adroit and very convincing.

A REVELATION.

But now we come to a very critical passage in Mr.
Pickwick's case : one that really destroyed any chance
that he had. It really settled the matter with the jury ;
and the worst was, the point was brought out through
the inefficiency of his own counsel.

But let us hear the episode, and see how the foolish
Phunky muddled it.

"Mr. Phunky rose for the purpose of getting something important out of Mr. Winkle in cross-examination. Whether he did get anything important out of
him, will immediately appear.

MR. PHUNKY.

'I believe, Mr. Winkle,' said Mr. Phunky, 'that Mr.
Pickwick is not a young man ? '

'Oh no,' replied Mr. Winkle, 'old enough to be my
father.'

'You have told my learned friend that you have
known Mr. Pickwick a long time. Had you ever any
reason to suppose or believe that he was about to be
married ? '

'Oh no; certainly not;' replied Mr. Winkle with so much eagerness, that Mr. Phunky ought to have got him out of the box with all possible dispatch. Lawyers hold out that there are two kinds of particularly bad witnesses, a reluctant witness, and a too willing witness ; it was Mr. Winkle's fate to figure in both characters.

'I will even go further than this, Mr. Winkle,' continued Mr. Phunky, in a most smooth and complacent manner. 'Did you ever see any thing in Mr. Pickwick's manner and conduct towards the opposite sex to induce you to believe that he ever contemplated matrimony of late years, in any case?'

'Oh no; certainly not,' replied Mr. Winkle.

'Has his behaviour, when females have been in the case, always been that of a man, who having attained a pretty advanced period of life, content with his own occupations and amusements, treats them only as a father might his daughters!'

'Not the least doubt of it,' replied Mr. Winkle, in the fulness of his heart. 'That is—yes—oh yes—certainly.'

'You have never known anything in his behaviour towards Mrs. Bardell, or any other female, in the least degree suspicious?' said Mr. Phunky, preparing to sit down, for Serjeant Snubbin was winking at him.

'N—n—no,' replied Mr. Winkle, 'except on one trifling occasion, which, I have no doubt, might be easily explained.'

"Now, if the unfortunate Mr. Phunky had sat down when Serjeant Snubbin winked at him, or if Serjeant Buzfuz had stopped this irregular cross-examination at the outset (which he knew better than to do, for observing Mr. Winkle's anxiety, and well knowing it would in all probability, lead to something serviceable to him), this unfortunate admission would not have been elicited. The moment the words fell from Mr. Winkle's lips, Mr.

Phunky sat down, and Serjeant Snubbin rather hastily
told him he might leave the box, which Mr. Winkle
prepared to do with great readiness, when Serjeant Buzfuz stopped him.

'Stay, Mr. Winkle—stay,' said Serjeant Buzfuz, ' will
your lordship have the goodness to ask him, what this
one instance of suspicious behaviour towards females on
the part of this gentlemen, who is old enough to be his
father, was ? '

'You hear what the learned counsel says, Sir,' observed
the Judge, turning to the miserable and agonized Mr.
Winkle.   'Describe the occasion to which you refer.'

'My lord,' said Mr. Winkle, trembling with anxiety,
'I—I'd rather not.'"   And Winkle had to relate the
whole Ipswich adventure of the doublebedded room and
the spinster lady.

It is surprising that Dodson and Fogg did not ferret
out all about Mr. Pickwick's adventure at the Great
White Horse.   Peter Magnus lived in town and must
have heard of the coming case ; these things *do* somehow leak out, and he would have gladly volunteered the
story, were it only to spite the man.   But further,
Dodson and Fogg must have made all sorts of enquiries
into Mr. Pickwick's doings.   Mrs. Bardell herself might
have heard something.   The story was certainly in the
Ipswich papers, for there was the riot in the street, the
appearance before the mayor, the exposure of " Captain
FitzMarshall "—a notable business altogether.   What
a revelation in open court !   Conceive Miss Witherfield called to depose to Mr. Pickwick's midnight in-
vasion.   Mr. Pickwick himself might have been called
and put on the rack, this incident not concerning his
breach of promise.   And supposing that the ubiquitous
Jingle had heard of this business and had gone to the
solicitor's office to volunteer evidence, and most useful
evidence it would have been—to wit that Mr. Pickwick

had been caught in the garden of a young ladies' school and had alarmed the house by his attempts to gain admission in the small hours! Jingle of course, could not be permitted to testify to this, but he could put the firm on the track. Mr. Pickwick's reputation could hardly have survived these two revelations, and sweeping damages to the full amount would have been the certain result.

This extraordinary adventure of Mr. Pickwick's at the Great White Horse Inn, Ipswich, verifies Dodson's casual remark to him, that " he was either a very designing or a most unfortunate man," circumstances being so strong against him. As the story was brought out, in open court, owing to the joint indiscretion of Phunky and Winkle, it will be best, in justice to Mr. Pickwick, to give practically his account of the affair.

" 'Nobody sleeps in the other bed, of course,' said Mr. Pickwick.

' Oh no, sir.'

' Very good. Tell my servant to bring me up some hot water at half-past eight in the morning, and that I shall not want him any more to night.'

' Yes, sir.' " And bidding Mr. Pickwick good-night, the chambermaid retired, and left him alone.

" Mr. Pickwick sat himself down in a chair before the fire, and fell into a train of rambling meditations. First he thought of his friends, and wondered when they would join him ; *then his mind reverted to Mrs. Martha Bardell;* and from that lady it wandered, by a natural process, to the dingy counting-house of Dodson and Fogg. From Dodson and Fogg's it flew off at tangent, to the very centre of the history of the queer client; and then it came back to the Great White Horse at Ipswich, with sufficient clearness to convince Mr. Pickwick that he was falling asleep: so he aroused himself, and began to undress, when he

recollected he had left his watch on the table down
stairs.   So as it was pretty late now, and he was un-
willing to ring his bell at that hour of the night, he
slipped on his coat, of which he had just divested
himself, and taking the japanned candlestick in his
hand, walked quietly down stairs.

"The more stairs Mr. Pickwick went down, the more
stairs there seemed to be to descend, and again and
again, when Mr. Pickwick got into some narrow passage,
and began to congratulate himself on having gained the
ground-floor, did another flight of stairs appear before his
astonished eyes.   At last he reached a stone hall, which
he remembered to have seen when he entered the house.
Passage after passage did he explore; room after room
did he peep into; at length, just as he was on the point
of giving up the search in despair, he opened the door
of the identical room in which he had spent the evening,
and beheld his missing property on the table.

"Mr. Pickwick seized the watch in triumph, and proceeded to retrace his steps to his bed-chamber.   If his
progress downwards had been attended with difficulties
and uncertainty, his journey back, was infinitely more
perplexing.   Rows of doors, garnished with boots of
every shape, make, and size, branched off in every possible direction.   A dozen times did he softly turn the
handle of some bedroom door, which resembled his own,
when a gruff cry from within of "Who the devil's that?"
or "What do want here?" caused him to steal away on
tiptoe, with a perfectly marvellous celerity.   He was
reduced to the verge of despair, when an open door
attracted his attention.   He peeped in—right at last.
There were the two beds, whose situation he perfectly
remembered, and the fire still buruing.   His candle, not
a long one when he first received it, had flickered away
in the drafts of air through which he had passed, and
sunk into the socket, just as he had closed the door after

him. 'No matter,' said Mr. Pickwick, ' I can undress myself just as well by the light of the fire.'

" The bedsteads stood, one each side of the door; and on the inner side of each, was a little path, terminating in a rush-bottomed chair, just wide enough to admit of a person's getting into, or out of bed, on that side if he or she thought proper. Having carefully drawn the curtains of his bed on the outside, Mr. Pickwick sat down on the rush-bottomed chair, and leisurely divested himself of his shoes and gaiters. He then took off and folded up, his coat, waistcoat, and neck-cloth, and slowly drawing on his tasseled night-cap, secured it firmly on his head, by tying beneath his chin, the strings which he always had attached to that article of dress. It was at this moment that the absurdity of his recent bewilderment struck upon his mind; and throwing himself back in the rush-bottomed chair, Mr. Pickwick laughed to himself so heartily, that it would have been quite delightful to any man of well-constituted mind to have watched the smiles which expanded his amiable features, as they shone forth, from beneath the night-cap.

'It is the best idea,' said Mr. Pickwick to himself, smiling till he almost cracked the night-cap strings— ' It is the best idea, my losing myself in this place, and wandering about those staircases, that I ever heard of. Droll, droll, very droll.' Here Mr. Pickwick smiled again, a broader smile than before, and was about to continue the process of undressing, in the best possible humour, when he was suddenly stopped by a most unexpected interruption; to wit, the entrance into the room of some person with a candle, who, after locking the door, advanced to the dressing table, and set down the light upon it.

" The smile that played upon Mr. Pickwick's features, was instantaneously lost in a look of the most unbounded and wonder-stricken surprise. The person, whoever it was, had come so suddenly and with so little noise, that Mr. Pickwick had had no time to call out, or oppose their entrance. Who could it be? A robber? Some evil-minded person who had seen him come upstairs with a handsome watch in his hand, perhaps. What was he to do!

" The only way in which Mr. Pickwick could catch a glimpse of his mysterious visitor with the least danger of being seen himself, was by creeping on to the bed, and peeping out from between the curtains on the opposite side. Keeping the curtains carefully closed with his hand, so that nothing more of him could be seen than his face and nightcap, and putting on his spectacles, he mustered up courage, and looked out.

" Mr. Pickwick almost fainted with horror and dismay. Standing before the dressing glass, was a middle-aged lady in yellow curl-papers, busily engaged in brushing what ladies call their " back hair." However the un-conscious middle-aged lady came into that room, it was quite clear that she contemplated remaining there for the night; for she had brought a rushlight and shade with her, which with praiseworthy precaution against fire, she had stationed in a basin on the floor, where it was glimmering away, like a gigantic lighthouse, in a particularly small piece of water.

'Bless my soul,' thought Mr. Pickwick, ' what a dreadful thing!'

'Hem!' said the lady; and in went Mr. Pickwick's head with automaton-like rapidity.

'I never met with anything so awful as this,'—thought poor Mr. Pickwick, the cold perspiration starting in drops upon his nightcap. 'Never. This is fearful.'

" It was quite impossible to resist the urgent desire to see what was going forward. So out went Mr. Pickwick's head again. The prospect was worse than before. The middle-aged lady had finished arranging her hair ; had carefully enveloped it, in a muslin nightcap with a small plaited border, and was gazing pensively on the fire.

'This matter is growing alarming'—reasoned Mr. Pickwick with himself. 'I can't allow things to go on

THE DOUBLE BEDDED ROOM,
GREAT WHITE HORSE, IPSWICH.

in this way. By the self-possession of that lady, it's clear to me that I must have come into the wrong room.

If I call out, she'll alarm the house, but if I remain here, the consequences will be still more frightful.'

" Mr. Pickwick, it is quite unnecessary to say, was one of the most modest and delicate-minded of mortals. The very idea of exhibiting his nightcap to a lady, overpowered him, but he had tied those confounded strings in a knot, and do what he would, he couldn't get it off. The disclosure must be made. There was only one other way of doing it. He shrunk behind the curtains, and called out very loudly—

'Ha—hum.'

" That the lady started at this unexpected sound was evident, by her falling up against the rushlight shade ; that she persuaded herself it must have been the effect of imagination was equally clear, for when Mr. Pickwick, under the impression that she had fainted away, stone-dead from fright, ventured to peep out again, she was gazing pensively on the fire as before.

'Most extraordinary female this,' thought Mr. Pickwick, popping in again. 'Ha—hum.'

" These last sounds, so like those in which, as legends inform us, the ferocious giant Blunderbore was in the habit of expressing his opinion that it was time to lay the cloth, were too distinctly audible, to be again mistaken for the workings of fancy.

'Gracious Heaven !' said the middle-aged lady, ' what's that !'

'It's—it's—only a gentleman, Ma'am,' said Mr. Pickwick from behind the curtains.

'A gentleman !' said the lady with a terriffc scream.

'It's all over,' thought Mr. Pickwick.

' A strange man,' shrieked the lady. Another instant and the house would be alarmed. Her garments rustled as she rushed towards the door.

'Ma'am,'—said Mr. Pickwick, thrusting out his head, in the extremity of desperation, 'Ma'am.'

"Now although Mr. Pickwick was not actuated by any definite object in putting out his head, it was instantaneously productive of a good effect. The lady, as we have alreaded stated, was near the door. She must pass it, to reach the staircase, and she would most undoubtedly have done so by this time, had not the sudden apparition of Mr. Pickwick's nightcap driven her back, into the remotest corner of the apartment, where she stood, staring wildly at Mr. Pickwick, while Mr. Pickwick, in his turn, stared wildly at her.

'Wretch,'—said the lady, covering her eyes with her hands, 'what do you want here.'

'Nothing, Ma'am—nothing whatever, Ma'am,' said Mr. Pickwick, earnestly.

'Nothing!' said the lady, looking up.

'Nothing, Ma'am, upon my honour,' said Mr. Pickwick, nodding his head so energetically, that the tassel of his nightcap danced again. 'I am almost ready to sink, Ma'am, beneath the confusion of addressing a lady in my nightcap (here the lady hastily snatched off her's), but I can't get it off, Ma'am (here Mr. Pickwick gave it a tremendous tug in proof of the statment). It is evident to me, Ma'am, now, that I have mistaken this bedroom for my own. I had not been here five minutes, Ma'am, when you suddenly entered it.'

'If this improbable story be really true, Sir,'—said the lady, sobbing violently, 'you will leave it instantly.'

'I will, Ma'am, with the greatest pleasure,' replied Mr. Pickwick.

'Instantly, Sir,' said the lady.

'Certainly, Ma'am,' interposed Mr. Pickwick very quickly. 'Certainly, Ma'am. I—I—am very sorry, Ma'am,' said Mr. Pickwick, making his appearance at the bottom of the bed, 'to have been the innocent occasion of this alarm and emotion; deeply sorry Ma'am.'

G

" The lady pointed to the door. One excellent quality
of Mr. Pickwick's character was beautifully displayed
at this moment, under the most trying circumstances.
Although he had hastily put on his hat over his night
cap, after the manner of the old patrol; although he
carried his shoes and gaiters in his hand, and his coat
and waistcoat over his arm, nothing could subdue his
native politeness.

' I am exceedingly sorry, Ma'am,' said Mr. Pickwick,
bowing very low.

' If you are, Sir, you will at once leave the room,' said
the lady.

' Immediately, Ma'am; this instant, Ma'am,' said
Mr. Pickwick, opening the door, and dropping both his
shoes with a loud crash in so doing.

' I trust Ma'am,' resumed Mr. Pickwick, gathering up
his shoes, and turning round to bow again, ' I trust,
Ma'am, that my unblemished character, and the devoted
respect I entertain for your sex, will plead as some slight
excuse for this '—But before Mr. Pickwick could con-
clude the sentence, the lady had thrust him into the
passage, and locked and bolted the door behind him.

" Whatever grounds of self-congratulation Mr. Pickwick might have, for having escaped so quietly from his
late awkward situation, his present position was by no
means enviable. He was alone, in an open passage, in a
strange house, in the middle of the night, half dressed;
it was not to be supposed that he could find his way in
perfect darkness to a room which he had been wholly
unable to discover with a light, and if he made the
slightest noise in his fruitless attempts to do so, he
stood every chance of being shot at, and perhaps killed,
by some wakeful traveller. He had no resource but to
remain where he was, until daylight appeared. So after
groping his way a few paces down the passage, and to
his infinite alarm, stumbling over several pairs of boots

in so doing, Mr. Pickwick crouched into a little recess in the wall, to wait for morning, as philosophically as he might.

" He was not destined, however, to undergo this additional trial of patience: for he had not been long ensconced in his present concealment when, to his unspeakable horror, a man, bearing a light, appeared at the end of the passage. His horror was suddenly converted into joy, however, when he recognized the form of his faithful attendant. It was indeed Mr. Samuel Weller, who after sitting up thus late, in conversation with the Boots, who was sitting up for the mail, was now about to retire to rest."

Imagine this story told by Miss Witherfield in open court, with all its details, the lady's narrative being coloured by the recollection that she had lost a suitable husband owing to her adventure. Mr. Peter Magnus would have deposed to Mr. Pickwick's extraordinary interest in the matter of the proposal, and have added his suspicions on recalling Mr. Pickwick's ambiguous declaration that he had come down to expose a certain person—even one of his own sympathetic friends, who had witnessed the scene with Mrs. Bardell, and recalled the Boarding House incident, might murmur, " How odd that he is ever thus in pursuit of the fair under suspicious circumstances? *could* it be that after all ?—What if he had some previous knowledge of the lady, and secretly admired her, and stung to fury at the notion of Mr. Peter Magnus marrying, had taken this strange mode of declaring his passion?" Even the sagacious Sam, devoted as he was to his master, was taken aback on meeting him in his midnight wanderings.

" ' Sam,' said Mr. Pickwick, suddenly appearing before him, ' Where's my bedroom ? '

" Mr. Weller stared at his master with the most emphatic surprise ; and it was not until the question had

been repeated three several times, that he turned round,
and led the way to the long-sought apartment.

'Sam,' said Mr. Pickwick, as he got into bed, 'I have
made one of the most extraordinary mistakes to-night,
that ever were heard of.'

'Werry likely, Sir,' replied Mr. Weller, drily.

'But of this I am determined, Sam,' said Mr. Pickwick, 'that if I were to stop in this house for six months,
I would never trust myself about it alone, again.'

'That's the wery prudentest resolution as you could
come to, Sir,' replied Mr. Weller. 'You rayther want
somebody to look arter you, Sir, ven your judgment
goes out a wisitin'.'

'What do you mean by that, Sam?' said Mr. Pickwick. He raised himself in bed, and extended his hand,
as if he were about to say something more; but suddenly checking himself, turned round, and bade his valet
'Good night.'

'Good night, Sir,' replied Mr. Weller. He paused
when he got outside the door—shook his head—walked
on—stopped—snuffed the candle—shook his head again
—and finally proceeded slowly to his chamber, appa-
ently buried in the profoundest meditation."

"It will be seen that Sam went near to being dis-
respectful in his sceptical view of his master's story.

When Mrs. Sanders was examined, "the Court" put
a few questions to her, as to the customs of love-making
among persons of her position. She had "received love
letters, like other ladies. In the course of their correspondence Mr. Sanders had often called her a 'duck' but
never 'chops' or 'tomato sauce.' He was particularly
fond of ducks. Perhaps if he had been as fond of chops
and tomato sauce, he might have called her that, as a
term of affection."

Mrs. Sanders was clearly one of the same class as Mrs.
Cluppins, and chiefly deposed to the general impression

in the neighbourhood that Mr. Pickwick had "offered" for Mrs. Bardell. Tupman, Snodgrass and Sam were also examined. Being friends of the defendant, they were from the outset assumed to be "hostile" and treated accordingly. It may be doubted, however, whether it is permissible to treat "your own witnesses" in this rough fashion, until at least they have shown some overt signs of their hostility, either by reserve, or an obvious determination to let as little as possible be extracted from them. In such case, it is usual to apply to the court for its sanction to deal with them by the severity of cross examination.

When Sam entered the witness box, the Serjeant addressed him : " I believe you are in the service of Mr. Pickwick, the Defendant in this case. *Speak up, if you please, Mr. Weller.*" Sam had not had time to say anything, so the admonition might seem superfluous. But this is a well-known device. Sam had been " briefed " to the Serjeant as a rather dangerous witness—somewhat too wide awake. It was necessary therefore to be short and summary with him. He thus conveyed to the jury that this Sam was one whom he could address in this curt way, and who by his low, uncertain accents might try to hide the truth. Sam, however, disconcerted the plan by his prompt, ready answer, " I *mean* to speak up, sir." Sam, as we know, clearly brought out the Dodson and Fogg's damaging assurance to Mrs. Bardell, that no costs should be charged to her personally.

When the Plaintiff's case was closed, things did not look particularly bright for Mr. Pickwick. It had been shown on the evidence of his own friends that he had been surprised with his landlady in his arms; (2) That he had been corresponding with her on most familiar terms—at least Serjeant Buzfuz had made it appear so ; (3) Language that *almost* amounted to a proposal had

been overheard; (4) And finally, it had been revealed
that the Defendant had been "caught" in a lady's
bedroom, at an Inn, at midnight! To answer which a
"strong" case was absolutely essential. This, we grieve
to say, was not forthcoming.

THE DEFENDANT'S CASE.

When we listen to the defence set up for Mr. Pickwick we have to lament that that worthy gentleman
was not better served by his legal advisers.

On the other side the shrewd Dodson and Fogg had
done admirably for their client.   They were sharp
clever attornies, having a thundering, overpowering
leader, and a smart, exceedingly smart junior, one of
those "wide-awake" brisk fellows who really conduct
the case, and will "take silk" in a few years.   This
gentleman could cross-examine in capital style and
address the jury in a language of his own, by glances,
shrugs, and remarks addressed to a witness, but intended
for the jury, as they knew perfectly well.   His style,
bearing, and speeches form an admirable epitome of the
arts and devices of a smart counsel.   There are "common" forms and Skimpin had them at his fingers' ends.
As we listen, we feel how admirably directed they were
to work on the jury.

Perker's plan of campaign as announced to Mr.
Pickwick, was a poor one enough, and showed how des-
perate he thought the case was.   "We have only one
(course) to adopt, my dear sir," he said, "cross-examine
the witnesses : trust to Snubbin's eloquence, throw dust
in the eyes of the judge, and ourselves on the jury."
Brave words, but nothing of the programme was carried
out.   The cross-examination of the witnesses was but
tamely attempted.   Snubbin's eloquence was not displayed beyond mildly praising his client's good character.   As for "throwing dust in the eyes of judge," we

have seen Mr. Justice Stareleigh was much too wide
awake for that; while the throwing themselves on the
jury was disastrous. There were several other lines of
defence which a more up-to-date solicitor would not
have overlooked. A less scrupulous man would have
made searching enquiries into Mrs. Bardell's history and
character; but his client, perhaps, would not have sanc-
tioned this course.

Perker is even absurd enough to talk of a *casa*, as
though it were some Italian word.

A *ca sa* was short for a writ of *Capias ad Satisfacien-
dum*, which gave a warrant to the officers to seize the
goods. There were various kinds of this machinery, but
what affected Mr. Pickwick was a *Capias ad Satisfacien-
dum*, to enforce attendance at the Court. The *ca sa* also
came after judgment, giving authority to imprison the
defendant till the claim was satisfied.

The appearance of such great guns as the two Serjeants is accounted for by a curious rule that Serjeants
only were permitted to lead in cases read in the Court
of Common Pleas.* This strange monopoly recalls
that other one, in the Court of Arches, where the advocates and judges used to exchange places and decide on
cases in which perhaps they had been advocates. These
illiberal and unaccountable restrictions have been swept
away, with the Courts themselves.

Very unusual indeed at this time was the appearance
of a lawyer of Serjeant Snubbin's class in court, and
there is a well-known story how, when Charles Butler
made his appearance on a special occasion, all the Bar
crowded in to hear him, and he had, I think, to get a
gown for the occasion.

One is sorry to think that there are no Serjeants now,

---

* Seven years after the Trial this monopoly was taken away from the
Serjeants—namely in 1834: then capriciously given back to them, and
finally abolished in 1840.

though at the Irish Bar there is one solitary survivor—
Serjeant Hemphill. Gone too, are their "coifs" and
other paraphernalia. With the abolition of the sepa-
rate courts they were found superfluous. We like to
hear of Serjeant Parry, Serjeant Ballantine, Serjeants
Warren and Talford, all four literary men.*

Having made this initial blunder, Perker did not even
instruct a good, smart and ready junior, but chose instead the incapable Phunky who really brought out that
fatal piece of evidence from Winkle, which " did for " his
case altogether. He had no business, as Boz tells us.

This junior, we are told, had been just called, that
is to say, he had been only eight years at the Bar.
Snubbin had never heard of him. The little judge, in
court, also said " that he never had the pleasure of
hearing the gentleman's name before," a sneer he would
not have ventured on to a counsel in good practice.
Snubbin's remark is amusing and sarcastic ; but now-a-
days any barrister who had been at the Bar eight years
would not be considered as just called, for if he has been
passed over for that time, he is likely never to make
a figure. The rude and unbecoming sneers, both of
Snubbin and the little Judge, seem amazing in our
present code of legal manners. Everything at that time,
however, was much more " in the rough " and coarser.
This was his first case ; and the poor creature is thus
described :

" Although an infant barrister, he was a full-grown
man. He had a very nervous manner, and a painful
hesitation in his speech ; it did not appear to be a
natural defect, but seemed rather the result of timidity,
arising from the consciousness of being " kept down "
by want of means, or interest, or connection, or impu-

---

* I have heard from the daughter of Mr. Chapman, the original publisher
of *Pickwick*, that Talfourd revised and directed the "Trial." On one occasion Boz was dining with him when the proof was brought in, with some
legal mistakes noted by Talfourd. Boz left the table and put it right.

dence, as the case might be. He was overawed by the
Serjeant, and profoundly courteous to the attorney.

'I have not had the pleasure of seeing you before,
Mr. Phunky,' said Serjeant Snubbin, with haughty con-
descension.

"Mr. Phunky bowed. He *had* had the pleasure of
seeing the Serjeant, and of envying him too, with all a
poor man's envy, for eight years and a quarter.

'You are with me in this case, I understand?' said
the Serjeant.

"If Mr. Phunky had been a rich man, he would have
instantly sent for his clerk to remind him; if he had
been a wise one, he would have applied his fore-finger
to his forehead, and endeavoured to recollect, whether,
in the multiplicity of his engagements he had under-
taken this one, or not; but as he was neither rich nor
wise (in this sense at all events) he turned red, and
bowed.

'Have you read the papers, Mr. Phunky?' inquired
the Serjeant.

"Here again, Mr. Phunky should have professed to
have forgotten all about the merits of the case; but as
he had read such papers as had been laid before him in
the course of the action, and had thought of nothing
else, waking or sleeping, throughout the two months
during which he had been retained as Mr. Serjeant
Snubbin's junior, he turned a deeper red, and bowed
again.

'This is Mr. Pickwick,' said the Serjeant, waving his
pen in the direction in which that gentleman was
standing.

"Mr. Phunky bowed to Mr. Pickwick with a reverence which a first client must ever awaken; and again
inclined his head towards his leader.

'Perhaps you will take Mr. Pickwick away,' said the
Serjeant, 'and—and—and—hear anything Mr. Pickwick

may wish to communicate. We shall have a consultation, of course.' With this hint that he had been interrupted quite long enough, Mr. Serjeant Snubbin, who had been gradually growing more and more abstracted, applied his glass to his eyes for an instant, bowed slightly round, and was once more deeply immersed in the case before him : which arose out of an interminable law suit, originating in the act of an individual, deceased a century or so ago, who had stopped up a pathway leading from some place which nobody ever came from, to some other place which nobody ever went to."

With such a pair the case was literally given away. Perker should have secured a man like the present Mr. Gill or Mr. Charles Matthews—they might have " broken down " the witnesses, or laughed the case out of court.

We may speculate—why did Perker make this foolish selection ? As to Snubbin there was some excuse, as it was the custom that Serjeants only should lead in the Court of Common Pleas. But for the choice of Phunky, Perker's stupidity alone was responsible.

Under these conditions Serjeant Snubbin's conduct of the case and his "handling" of the witnesses was truly inefficient. He lost every opportunity for helping his client. He " led " in a quiet, gentlemanly and almost indifferent way. His first opportunity came in examining Mrs. Cluppins. As we have seen, she had deposed to hearing, when the door was " on the jar," Mr. Pickwick make those speeches which Mrs. Bardell had taken to be a proposal. Now here was the moment to show the ambiguity and that Mr. Pickwick was speaking of his servant. It might have been brought out that Sam was actually engaged that day, and that she had met him on the stairs, etc. But Snubbin declined to ask her a single question, saying that Mr. Pickwick admitted

the accuracy of her statement.   But this was beside the
matter, and the Serjeant need not have impeached her
accuracy.

When Phunky came to Winkle, the inexperience of
the tyro was shown at once.   Again, here was the
moment to have extracted from the witness a full explanation of Mr. Pickwick's ambiguous speeches to Mrs.
Bardell.   He could have " brought out" as " clear as
the light of day" that Mr. Pickwick was speaking of
his engagement of a valet and have shown that the valet
was to be engaged that very morning.   It would have
been impossible to resist such an explanation.   But the
thing was not thought of.   From him also could have
been drawn a vast deal favourable to Mr. Pickwick such
as his disgust and annoyance at Mrs. Baredll's behaviour,
his wish to be rid of her, his complaints of her conduct.
But no, there was only the foolish question as to Mr.
Pickwick's being an elderly man and of fatherly ways,
a topic that would by no means negative the presump-
tion of matrimony.   But nothing could excuse the
rashness of putting a general question as to " Mr. Pickwick's behaviour towards females."   No adroit counsel
would run the risk of encountering a too conscientious
witness, such as Winkle proved to be and who would
" let the cat out of the bag."

As we have seen, this awkward question settled Mr.
Pickwick's business.   Snubbin had held him out as an
elderly but benevolent being, treating every female he
met as a daughter, never dreaming of matrimony: when
lo ! the whole fabric is overthrown in an instant by the
luckless Winkle's admission !

" Amid the profound silence of the whole court Mr.
Winkle faltered out that the trifling circumstance of
suspicion was Mr. Pickwick's being found in a lady's
sleeping apartment at midnight, which had terminated,
he believed, in breaking off the projected marriage of the

lady, and had led, *he knew*, to the whole party being forcibly carried before a magistrate."

Thus was the defendant suddenly revealed as a Pecksniffian Lothario, and his pretence of philanthrophy after was shewn in its true colours. It was impossible not to associate this with the scene with Mrs. Bardell.

But there was an important legal " point" which one might have expected would have occurred to so eminent a Chamber Counsel as Serjeant Snubbin. To prove a breach of the promise, it must always be shown that the defendant had been given an opportunity of officially refusing to fulfil it. It should have been put to him " in black and white," " Will you marry me ? " and he must have answered "No, I will not," or something to that effect. In default of this the defendant might plead " True I gave the promise and it stands unbroken, for you never required me to act upon it." Now in Mr. Pickwick's case this actually occurred. As we have seen he left town the morning after the imputed proposal and while he was away, within a month, the notice of action was sent to him. Up to that time he had not heard a word of Dodson and Fogg, or of legal proceedings. But it may be urged that Mrs. Bardell herself may have written, formulating her demands. That this was not the case is evident from Mr. Pickwick's behaviour ; he did not dream of such a thing, or he would have been disturbed by it, or have consulted his friends about it. Had it been so, his high opinion of Mrs. Bardell would have been shattered. For did he not say on seeing Dodson and Fogg's letter, " She couldn't do it, she hasn't the heart to do it." The only thing that makes against this theory is his reply to Peter Magnus who asked him " had he ever proposed ? " when he answered vehemently " Never," possibly recalling Mrs. Bardell. She may however have written to him a pleading letter reminding him of what he had said to her, declaring her deep-

seated affection for him and inviting him to carry out
what he had offered. Mr. Pickwick would have replied
in one of his amiable letters, couched in rather general
terms, perhaps calling her "my dear creature," but putting aside the whole business: and there the matter
probably dropped for a time. I have little doubt the
good woman up to the last really believed that her
elderly lodger intended to make her an offer of his hand,
and that on his return from his travels he would resume
the business. Much elated by this prospect, and most
naturally too, she had told all her friends and neighbours of her approaching advancement. This Mrs.
Sanders specially deposed to: "had always said and believed that Pickwick would marry Mrs. Bardell; knew
that Mrs. Bardell being engaged to Pickwick was the
current topic of conversation in the neighbourhood, after
the fainting in July; had been told it herself by Mrs.
Mudberry which kept a mangle, and Mrs. Bunkin which
clear-starched, but did not see either Mrs. Mudberry or
Mrs. Bunkin in court."

Notwithstanding these speculations, it still does not
appear that Pickwick made such a legal and official re-
fusal to execute his promise as would be sufficient to
support the statement of what is now called "the sum-
mons and plaint," to wit, that the plaintiff being able
and willing "to marry the defendant the defendant refused, etc."

There is another matter on which hands of skilful
counsel might have affected Mrs. Bardell and which my
friend Mr. Burnand ("F. C. B.") was the first to push
home. At the trial, Mrs. Saunders cross-examined by
Serjeant Snubbin, had to admit that her friend had an
admirer—a certain Baker in the neighbourhood—who
was supposed to have matrimonial designs. Pressed on
this matter she thus deposed: "Had heard Pickwick
ask the little boy how he should like to have another

father. Did not know that Mrs. Bardell was at that time keeping company with the baker, but did know that the baker was then a single man, and is now married. Couldn't swear that Mrs. Bardell was not very fond of the baker, but should think that the baker was not very fond of Mrs. Bardell, or he wouldn't have married somebody else. Thought Mrs. Bardell fainted away on the morning in July, because Pickwick asked her to name the day; knew that she (witness) fainted away stone dead when Mr. Saunders asked *her* to name the day, and believed that everybody as called herself a lady would do the same, under similar circumstances. Heard Pickwick ask the boy the question about the marbles, but upon her oath did not know the difference between an alley tor and a commoney.

By the COURT.—During the period of her keeping company with Mr. Sanders, had received love letters, like other ladies. In course of their correspondence Mr. Sanders had often called her a 'duck,' but never 'chops,' nor yet 'tomata sauce.' He was particularly fond of ducks. Perhaps if he had been as fond of chops and tomata sauce, he might have called her that, as a term of affection.

What a point, too, Serjeant Snubbin missed here! Could he not have quoted the old verses. How he would have convulsed the court as he poured out the apropos "for Tommy and Me!"

> Pat-a-cake, Pat-a-cake, baker's man,
>   Bake me a cake as quick as you can;
> Knead it and bake it as fast as can be,
>   And put in the oven for Tommy and me.

Now we do not find that the Serjeant made any use of this topic in his speech. He might have surely urged that this "wily and experienced widow" was eager for a husband, that having been "thrown over" by her baker and stung by the mortification, she resolved, as it were, to rehabilitate herself and prepare this "plant" for her unsuspecting lodger. As Sir Henry Irving says in the play, "I don't like widows; *they know too much.*" F. C. B., as I have said, has treated this baker theme and developed it regularly in his amusing operetta "Pickwick."

The little epitome given of Snubbin's speech shows how weak were his topics, and that he, in fact, considered that there was no defence.

"Serjeant Snubbin then addressed the jury on behalf of the defendant; and a very long and a very emphatic address he delivered, in which he bestowed the highest possible eulogiums on the conduct and character of Mr. Pickwick. He attempted to show that the letters which had been exhibited, merely related to Mr. Pickwick's dinner, or to the preparations for receiving him in his apartments on his return from some country excursion. It is sufficient to add in general terms, that he did the best he could for Mr. Pickwick; and the best, as everybody knows on the infallible authority of the old adage, could do no more." This was no more than speaking "in mitigation of damages."

Mr. Phunky made no speech, which was just as well, as he might have but damaged the case, as no witnesses had been called on his side. For the same reason, the Court had not the pleasure of hearing Skimpin, who would no doubt have "torn the Defendant's case to tatters."

CHARGE AND VERDICT.

The regular formula is this. The judge begins to read his notes, and makes "running comments" as he goes along. "We have first, gentlemen, the statement of Mrs. Cluppins, she tells you, &c. Of course she comes as the friend of the Plaintiff, and naturally takes a favourable view of her case. If you are satisfied with her statement, it is for you, gentlemen, to consider what value you will attach to it. Then we come to the question of damages. This is entirely a matter for you. You must take into account the position in life of the Defendant, and what the Plaintiff has lost by his default. On the other hand they must be reasonable in amount. If you believe the promise has been clearly established, you should give substantial though not excessive damages, on a scale sufficient to repay the Plaintiff for the wrong. On the other hand—should it seem to you doubtful whether the promise had been made—you will give the Defendant the benefit of the doubt. These are questions entirely for you--not for me. On the whole case, you will ask yourselves, whether a promise such as would satisfy reasonable men, has been supported by sufficient evidence. If so, Plaintiff is entitled to damages —on the other hand, if this is not proved to your satisfaction, you will find for the Defendant."

Mr. Justice Stareleigh, however, as we are told, then "summed up in his old established and most approved form. He read as much of his notes as he could decypher on so short a notice, and made running comments

on the evidence as he went along. If Mrs. Bardell were
right, it was perfectly clear that Mr. Pickwick was
wrong, and if they thought the evidence of Mrs. Cluppins worthy of credence, they would believe it, and if
they didn't, why they would'nt. If they were satisfied
that a breach of promise had been committed, they
would find for the Plaintiff, with such damages as they
thought proper; and if, on the other hand, it appeared
to them that no promise of marriage had ever been
given, they would find for the Defendant, with no damages at all." Such was this lucid direction—which is
really, not in the least, an exaggeration.

But I could fancy some acute judge of our time—such
as Mr. Justice Day or Mr. Justice Bigham—after trying
this case, turning round in his seat to "charge" the
jury. "Here, gentlemen," he would tell them, "we have
it claimed on one side that a promise of marriage was
made—and broken; on the other hand the Defendant
denies having ever given such a promise. The question
you will have to deal with is: What was this promise,
and when was it given? In other words, *when* did the
Defendant propose to the lady. On the part of the
Plaintiff, this was said to have been done at the interview in Goswell Street, and two friends of the Plaintiff—
Mrs. Cluppins, I think"—turning over his notes—"yes,
Cluppins, and Sanders both declare positively that
they overheard the language of the proposal. Further,
Mr. Pickwick's friends are called, to prove that the lady
was in his arms, fainting. It is extraordinary that not
one of these three gentlemen should have deposed to any
statements or have offered explanations of the situation.
One witness indeed says that he heard the Defendant
remonstrate with the Plaintiff, on her hysterical behaviour, and ask her to consider that if any one should
come in, what would be said. Now, this is not the language of an ardent suitor, who would rather wish than

otherwise, that such endearing familiarities should continue : though I don't think you need seriously accept the reading the learned Counsel, Mr. Skimpin, put on the phrase used ; on the other hand, the words ' my dear creature,' were distinctly heard.

" There is one little incident," the Judge might go on, " which I must not pass by, and which is not without its significance. A witness deposed that the defendant was noted for his kindness to the Plaintiff's little boy—that he was constantly giving him presents, and once was heard to say to him, patting him on the head, ' *how would you like to have another father ?* ' Now, this addressed to a child of tender years does seem an odd sort of speech. Of course, it will be contended that the reference was to the probability of his Mother marrying some one other than the Defendant : if that be the case, it seems to me rather an indelicate and reckless speech. And then it must be said, it seems inconsistent with the amiable and benevolent character given to the Defendant to-day. On the other hand, if he were referring to *himself* it will appear natural and proper enough. And there is this to be added, that when the child had reported the remark to his mother, which of course he did, she would most reasonably begin to found hopes upon it. And then what follows, Gentlemen ?—the Defendant is found holding this lady in his arms, and becomes so demonstrative in his attentions that this very child comes to her rescue. I am inexperienced in these things—they may be innocent and done with the purest intentions, or may not ; but you, Gentlemen of the Jury, are men of the world : and it is for you to put the proper construction on them."

" You will have noted, Gentlemen, this curious feature of the case. None of the witnesses were in the room when the imputed proposal was made, yet all, Cluppins, Weller, and the Defendant's three friends, *heard* what

the Defendant said. This suggests that he must have
been very pressing, if not agitated. One of the witnesses, Winkle, I think, yes, Winkle, actually deposes to
hearing the words, 'My dear creature! Compose yourself' and the like. He added he was afraid someone
might come in; a very reasonable fear, Gentlemen, and
well grounded : for several persons *did* come in and it
would seem with awkward results for the Defendant.
But, Gentlemen, I confess that what most of all weighs
with me in this case is the remarkable avowal wrung
from a reluctant witness, of the Defendant's being surprised at midnight in a lady's bed-chamber, and being
taken, after a serious riot, before the Magistrates.
This came on me, as I saw it did on you all, as a surprise.
True, it does not bear on the question of a promise or
of the breach. But still it seems a matter which you
cannot wholly shut out from your consideration. It
startled me as it did you, to find a sort of travelling
philanthropist, as the Defendant Pickwick holds himself
out to be, on whose mildly benevolent features nature
seems to have stamped rectitude and high principle, living a life of hypocrisy, taking part in midnight invasions
and daylight riots. It is one of his own friends who
tells us this sad story : and it is for you to consider
whether the Plaintiff was here also in pursuit of yet
another disreputable game, holding out marriage as the
bait : I seem to speak strongly, but I feel it would be
impossible to withdraw this from your consideration.

"You may reasonably ask yourselves of what Pickwick was afraid—or why did he dread the presence of
witnesses ? Was he simply beguiling the lady, as he attempted to beguile that lady at Ipswich, without
'meaning business,' as the phrase runs. I must say the
Plaintiff had rather reasonable grounds for assuming
that the Defendant *did* mean business. But all this is
for you, Gentlemen, not for me.

" Then we have the man Weller's statement—a sort of humorous stage servant, not unamusing— and of course entirely devoted to his master's interest. I don't think you need attach any importance to what he said of the solicitors for the Plaintiff. When I was at the Bar, Gentlemen, attornies did much worse things than this."

The jury consulted for only a few minutes. Perhaps, however, they were only discussing the amount of damages. They were certainly moderate—laid at £1500 —though had Dodson and Fogg's advice prevailed, it should have been double. This only, by the way, is further proof of the amiable Mrs. Bardell's moderation and secret *tendre* for her genial lodger. Considering that Mr. Pickwick was 'a gentleman,' and further a gentleman of means, and that Mrs. Bardell was but an humble lodging-house keeper, the sum seems hardly commensurate. Dodson and Fogg no doubt expected £1,000.

" An anxious quarter of an hour elapsed ; the jury came back ; the judge was fetched in. Mr. Pickwick put on his spectacles, and gazed at the foreman with an agitated countenance and a quickly beating heart.

" ' Gentlemen,' said the individual in black, ' are you all agreed upon your verdict ? '

' We are,' replied the foreman.

' Do you find for the plaintiff, gentlemen, or for the defendant ? '

' For the plaintiff.'

' With what damages, gentlemen ? '

' Seven hundred and fifty pounds.' "

" Mr. Pickwick took off his spectacles, carefully wiped the glasses, folded them into their case, and put them in his pocket ; then having drawn on his gloves with great nicety, and stared at the foreman all the while, he mechanically followed Mr. Perker and the blue bag out of court.

"They stopped in a side room while Perker paid the court fees; and here, Mr. Pickwick was joined by his friends. Here, too, he encountered Messrs. Dodson and Fogg, rubbing their hands with every token of outward satisfaction.

" 'Well, gentlemen,' said Mr. Pickwick.

'Well, sir,' said Dodson: for self and partner.

'You imagine you'll get your costs, don't you, gentlemen?' said Mr. Pickwick.

"Fogg said they thought it rather probable. Dodson smiled, and said they'd try.

'You may try, and try, and try again, Messrs. Dodson and Fogg,' said Mr. Pickwick vehemently, 'but not one farthing of costs or damages do you ever get from me, if I spend the rest of my existence in a debtor's prison.'

'Ha, ha!' laughed Dodson. 'You will think better of that, before next term, Mr. Pickwick.'

'He, he, he!' We'll soon see about that Mr. Pickwick,' grinned Mr. Fogg.

"Speechless with indignation, Mr. Pickwick allowed himself to be led by his solicitor and friends to the door, and there assisted into a hackney-coach, which had been fetched for the purpose, by the ever watchful Sam Weller.

"Sam had put up the steps; and was preparing to jump upon the box, when he felt himself gently touched on the shoulder; and looking round, his father stood before him. The old gentleman's countenance wore a mournful expression, as he shook his head gravely, and said, in warning accents:

'I know'd what 'ud come 'o this here mode 'o doin' bisness. Oh Sammy, Sammy, vy worn't there a alleybi!'"

We may wonder that the laborious Chamber Counsel Serjeant Snubbin did not advise "moving for a new trial." The verdict was clearly a wrong one—no sufficient evidence had been furnished either of a promise, or a breach. The full court would no doubt have granted the motion, and this would have led to Mr. Pickwick's release, for the astute Dodson and Fogg must have recognised their poor chances, and perhaps have required "security for costs," which their client could not have given. However, the idea did not occur to anybody.

Since the law was changed both plaintiff and defendant may be examined in such cases as these. What a different complexion this would have put on the suit. The whole case would have tumbled to pieces like a pack of cards. For Mr. Pickwick "put into the box" would have clearly shown that all that had been thus misconstrued, was his proposal for engaging a valet, which was to have been that very morning. He would have related the words of the dialogue, and the Jury would have seen at once how the mistake arose. On the other hand, he would have been exposed to a severe rating cross examination by the learned Serjeant—fortified by Winkle's most damaging slip about the White Horse incident—who would have forced out of him all the incidents. We can almost hear the Serjeant subject the Defendant to the torture.

"This fellow of yours, Sir, was he recommended to you by a friend?"

"No—not at all."

"By a Registry Office?"

"Certainly not—nothing of the kind."

"Nothing of the kind? I suppose too low a class of place for you, eh? Come Sir!"

"I never said such a thing."

"Nor thought it, I suppose? Come, Sir, no beating about the bush. In plain terms, did you get him from a low Public House in the Boro'?"

Mr. Pickwick started up.

"Never!"

" Do you deny it ? "

" I never knew that the White Hart was a low Public House," said the witness indignantly.

" Never mind what you know, Sir. Did you or did you not get him from there ? " thundered the Serjeant.

" Of course I did."

" Of course you did. Then what's the use of all this juggling. It does you no good with My Lord and the Jury. I tell you plainly, Mr. Pickwick, we mean to have all out of you. Now Sir, was this man of yours an experienced valet ? "

" Certainly not."

" He had, of course, some training in his profession in other families ? "

" Not that I know of."

" Not that you know of. Do you dare to persist in that, Sir ? "

" Why not ? "

" Don't ask *me* questions, Sir, I'm asking *you*. Do you deny, Sir, that the man was neither more nor less than a common Boots in the yard of a Public House, wearing an old tattered hat and jacket—very different from the suit in which you have rigged him up here to-day ? "

Mr. Pickwick was astonished and silent. He was suffering. He had never dreamed of this view.

" Why," he said, " I suppose—"

" We want none of your supposes, Sir, answer yes or no."

" Well he certainly was such as you describe."

A flutter ran round the court.

" And this creature of yours, you would impose on the Jury as a trained man servant. You may go down Sir."

PLEA FOR "DODSON AND FOGG."

This famous firm of city attornies has become a bye-word in legal history—being considered the most notorious of practitioners for sharp, underhand, scheming practices. Boz was always vehement against the abuses of the law, but his generous ardour sometimes led him to exaggerated and wholesale statements that were scarcely well founded. This is found in some degree even in the sweeping attacks in *Bleak House*. But he was so vivid, so persuasive, in his pictures, that there was no appeal.

The unreasoning fury of Mr. Pickwick is specially shown in the case of Jingle, whom he pursued with an animosity that was almost frantic. One would think it was some public enemy he was hunting down for the public good. Poor Jingle had really done nothing so monstrous, after all. He had " chaffed " Dr. Slammer, "run off" with the spinster aunt—nothing so uncommon in those days—had been consigned to the Fleet for non-payment of his debts, and there showed penitence and other signs of a good heart. His one serious offence was passing himself off as a naval officer, and under an assumed name. But he had *crossed* Mr. Pickwick—had ridiculed him—had contemptuously sent a message to " Tuppy." When he dared to play a practical joke on his persecutor, his infamy passed beyond bounds. Here was the key to Mr. Pickwick's nature—any lack of homage or respect was an offence against morality. So with Dodson and Fogg. He had settled in his mind that a condescending visit to these gentlemen, with a little explanation and remonstrance would completely disarm them. His fury on his advances being rejected was extraordinary.

Here Boz shows, as he ever does, his profound and most logical treatment of human character. He never goes astray, being guided by a happy and true instinct. Mr. Pickwick had grown to be the most inflated of men. Flattered and followed—submitted to with the greatest deference—ordering people about—doing what he pleased —he could not stand the slightest opposition. No one was to contradict—no one to question even his stockings —speckled or others. Even when he was clearly wrong, it was an affront to hint at it. He had much in common with that great man, Mr. Gladstone, who was the political Pickwick of his time. He was overbearing and arrogant and unrestrained, and I am afraid vindictive. Dodson and Fogg were associated with the great mortification of his life. He could not forgive them—the very sight of them roused his hatred, and the having to pay them ransom stung him to fury. All which is most natural and yet unexpected.

The popular and genial Sir Frank Lockwood was almost the first to put forward a plea in abatement of prejudice for the firm. He showed that they were not much below the usual type of middle-class solicitors. What they did was in the ordinary course. With Mr. Pickwick they were most forbearing, and even indulgent. There was one rather doubtful passage, but even here he offers extenuation. This was their treatment of poor Ramsey, which, at first sight, seems very bad indeed.

" 'There was such a game with Fogg here, this mornin',' said the man in the brown coat, 'while Jack was upstairs sorting the papers, and you two were gone to the stamp-office. Fogg was down here opening the letters, when that chap we issued the writ against at

Camberwell, you know, came in—what's his name
again ? '

'Ramsey,' said the clerk who had spoken to Mr.
Pickwick.

'Ah, Ramsey—a precious seedy-looking customer.
'Well, sir,' says old Fogg, looking at him very fierce—
you know his way—'well, Sir, have you come to settle ? '
'Yes, I have, Sir,' said Ramsey, putting his hand in his
pocket, and bringing out the money, 'the debt two
pound ten, and the costs three pound five, and here it
is, sir ; ' and he sighed like bricks, as he lugged out the
money, done up in a bit of blotting paper.   Old Fogg
looked first at the money, and then at him, and then
he coughed in his rum way, so that I knew something
was coming.   'You don't know there's a declaration
filed, which increases the costs materially, I suppose ?
said Fogg.   'You don't say that Sir,' said Ramsey,
starting back ; 'the time was only out last night, Sir,'
'I do say it, though,' said Fogg, 'my clerk's just gone
to file it.   Hasn't Mr. Jackson gone to file that declaration in Bullman and Ramsey, Mr. Wicks ? '   Of course
I said yes, and then Fogg coughed again, and looked at
Ramsey.   'My God !' said Ramsey ; 'and here have I
nearly driven myself mad, scraping this money together,
and all to no purpose.'   'None at all,' said Fogg, coolly ;
'so you had better go back and scrape some more
together, and bring it here in time.'   'I can't get it, by
God,' said Ramsey, striking the desk with his fist.
'Don't bully me, Sir,' said Fogg, getting into a passion
on purpose.   'I am not bullying you, Sir,' said Ramsey.
'You are,' said Fogg ; 'get out, Sir, get out of this
office, Sir, and come back, Sir, when you know how to
behave yourself.'   Well, Ramsey tried to speak, but
Fogg wouldn't let him, so he put the money in his
pocket, and sneaked out.   The door was scarcely shut,
when old Fogg turned round to me, with a sweet smile on

his face, and drew the declaration out of his coat pocket.
' Here, Wick's, says Fogg, ' take a cab, and go down to
the Temple as quick as you can, and file that.   The costs
are quite safe, for he's a steady man with a large family,
at a salary of five-and-twenty shillings a week, and if he
gives us a warrant of attorney, as he must in the end, I
know his employers will see it paid; so we may as well
get all we can out of him, Mr. Wicks; it's a Christian
act to do it, Mr. Wicks, for with his large family and
small income, he'll be all the better for a good lesson
against getting into debt,—won't he, Mr. Wicks, won't
he?'—and he smiled so goodnaturedly as he went away,
that it was delightful to see him.   He is a capital man
of business,' said Wicks, in a tone of the deepest admiration, ' capital, isn't he?'

" The other three cordially subscribed to this opinion,
and the anecdote afforded the most unlimited satisfaction.

' Nice men these here, Sir,' whispered Mr. Weller to
his master; ' very nice notion of fun they has, Sir."

Sir F. Lockwood, by the way, offers one of the most
amusing proofs conceivable, of the convincing power of
" Pickwick," which is constantly taking us out of the
world of fiction, into that of the daily living life.   He
speaks of the cruel trick played upon the unfortunate
Ramsey, who came to pay his bill of costs, and was told
that these were out of date, had been swelled by
subsequent proceedings.   An affidavit had been sworn
—which, after he left the house, Wicks, the clerk, was
sent off to swear—Then, Sir Frank, adds : " After all,
this is merely given *as the statement of Wicks—on whose
testimony not much reliance can be placed.*"   As though
Wicks were some living witness, " erect upon two legs,"
whom he had been examining in Court !

It must, however, be recollected that this was an *ex-
parte* story.   Wicks, as Sir F. Lockwood hints, may

have coloured it up, to amuse his brethren. The truth is these poor helpless debtors, who fall into the hands of legal " sharks " and money-lenders, have *their* tricks also. They will often " do " those they employ if they can. And further, let this be considered. Before Ramsey paid his visit the affidavit *had* been prepared, and was actually in Fogg's pocket. Such affidavit would not be allowed for in the costs unless necessary to the case, so that Fogg's statement that it had been filed was very near the truth. Perker himself was play-ing the same game of hide and seek with another unfortunate—one Watty—who was trying to see him, and learn something about his case, but was always put off with the excuse or falsehood, that Perker was out, though he was within. But then, "Perker was an honourable man."

Boz lets us know, through Sam, how the case reached Dodson and Fogg. He speaks of " the kind generous people o' the perfession 'as sets their clerks to work to find out little disputes among their neighbours and ac-quaintances as wants settlin' by means of law suits." This system, however, cannot be checked, and " the speculative attorney " even in our time still flourishes.

It was really not a question whether Mr. Pickwick would " indict them for a conspiracy," because they acted as solicitors against him, but whether they would bring an action against *him* on their own account. All through, Mr. Pickwick's behaviour to them had been outrageous. He chose to assume, quite gratuitously that it was they—not Mrs. Bardell—who got up the case; that they had worked on her for their own nefarious ends. Nothing could be more absurd. The landlady was eager enough to protect her own interests —her female friends worked on her, and the loss of so valuable a lodger, which the incident must have entailed, inflamed her more. We can see from Sam's interview

with her that she was at last, though at first reluctant,
determined to have her rights. But Mr. Pickwick
acting on this assumption addressed the firm, from the
first to the last in the most scurrilous language. He
called them "robbers, swindlers,—a brace of pettifogging scoundrels!" Shocking and ungentlemanly terms,
and what is worse, actionable. Yet the pair received
this abuse with infinite good temper and restraint,
merely securing a witness who should listen, and threatening the speaker with legal penalties.

And why did they not take this course? Well, they
had to suspend proceedings until Mrs. Bardell's action
was settled, when on receiving their costs they were
desirous to part in good humour. But Mr. Pickwick
was so furious at being invited to shake hands with
them, that he again broke out with coarse abuse,
"Robbers!" "Robbers!" calling it after them down
the stairs. Why did they not take action on this?
Perhaps they were afraid; as Mr. Pickwick had shewn
himself such a doughty and unyielding fighter—going
to prison rather than pay. Perhaps they thought he
might get the better of them again.

We have very little evidence as to what was the scale
of fees in use in these days. They were of course far
lower than they are now, after allowances even for
the lower cost of living. To-day, the fees to Counsel
alone would have absorbed considerably more than
Dodson and Fogg's whole bill of costs. A nice point
is, could Mr. Pickwick's irregular interview with Serjeant Snubbin be considered something in the way of a
consultation? Here were Counsel, Solicitor and Client:
the Serjeant gave up a portion of his valuable time and,
further, the junior counsel was summoned specially from
his chambers to supply his "advice and opinion." Mr.
Pickwick ought surely to have to pay for his whim.

And the bill of costs that these "sharks" of attornies

sent in! It was astonishingly moderate. For writ, service of subpœnas, hunting up evidence, consultation, fees to counsel, fees for the day, retainers, etc.,—the sum of £120 was all that was asked.

Imagine Messrs. Lewis and Lewis sending in such a demand at the end of a trial which it had taken them nearly a year to get ready. In our time it could hardly be done under £1,000. Perker, by the way, told his client that on payment of the costs both of Plaintiff and Defendent, into the hands of " these sharks " he would get his release. With much indulgence—the attornies —allowed him to leave the prison on his bare undertaking to pay. And it is not clear why he should pay his own costs to them, and not to Perker. And they were *not* paid for sometime. Mr. Pickwick's own costs must have been small. He had no witnesses. Perker would not have made a hand of him, and I fancy he would have got off for ninety pounds, or a hundred pounds. There was, however, the fees of the Special Jury, so he would have to pay, say, £220.

THE COGNOVIT.

Perker, it has been shown, was not a very brilliant solicitor, and his views on the trial were somewhat cloudy. When he was urging his client to leave the Fleet he threw out some equally shadowy and ill-informed notions as to what might be done in the way of punishing the nefarious solicitors, Dodson and Fogg, "those Freeman's Court Sharks."

His great charge was that they had got a *cognovit*, or undertaking to pay their costs out of Mrs. Bardell— their own client! Mr. Pickwick refused to pay them— why should not she? The poor woman had "blabbed" to Sam, a careless and natural assurance of theirs, that they would be content to get them from Mr. Pickwick —a thing many a firm would do. But Perker here sees a regular conspiracy. "I cannot undertake to say whether the wording of the cognovit, the nature of the ostensible consideration and the proof we can get together about the whole conduct of the suit, *will be sufficient to justify an indictment for conspiracy.*"

It is impossible to understand this bit of legal jargon. "The wording of the cognovit"—one could speculate on *that* without seeing it. (2) "The nature of the ostensible consideration" was not far to seek—it being work and labour done for the Plaintiff. And again, supposing they had promised her to get them solely from Mr. Pickwick—Sam's revelation of this, in open court, and its reception with laughter, showed what was thought of it. So which of the two courses were they to adopt? (3) And "the proof we may get together about the whole conduct of the suit." This "whole conduct" was perfectly regular. So the Judge thought— so did the jury. The case was proved by Pickwick's own friends. As we know, however, the firm took no steps to obtain satisfaction, but there cannot be the slightest doubt that they would have "recovered damages." We doubt if Mr. Pickwick would have gone to the Fleet for the second time rather than pay.

Perker's suspicions as to the *Cognovit* obtained by Dodson and Fogg were shrewd, and certain enough, though he could not have seen the document. The suspicions were well warranted by the state of the Law, which became an instrument in the hands of grasping attorneys. By it the client was made to sign an acknow- ledgment, and offering no defence to a supposed action, —say for costs—brought against him, Judgment was then marked.

This offered a great temptation to the unscrupulous. Mrs. Bardell, no doubt, signed with light heart, not knowing what she was doing, and being told that it was merely a matter of form. Various enactments attempted to protect the client—one being passed some four or five years before the trial Bardell v. Pickwick, requiring the *Cognovit* to be regularly filed within twenty-one days; more than ten years later it was required, that the client's signing such a thing should have no force in Law, unless he was represented by another solicitor.

The matter, as we know, was compromised with Dodson and Fogg, so there was no need to scrutinize the *Cognovit*. No doubt Perker was enabled to put pressure on the firm by hinting at such proceedings.

The damages, £750, were certainly moderate, and would not have been reduced by the Court on an ap- plication to set them aside as "excessive." The good woman was quite at her ease, being no doubt certain

I

that Mr. Pickwick, at last, must give in. She could
even enjoy the society of her friends and make the
celebrated junketting to the "Spaniards." The firm
took another view and grew tired of waiting; or they
were sagacious enough to see that the arrest of their
client was about the best method of putting pressure on
Mr. Pickwick. In this connection, it may be noted that
Jackson's over zeal in the transaction might have led to
an action against his employers; for he arrested not
only Mrs. Bardell, but her friends, Mrs. Sanders and
Mrs. Cluppins. The prison gates were actually shut on
them. "Safe and sound," said the Bailiff. "Here we
are at last," said Jackson, "all right and tight."

True, Mrs. Bardell put under her hand in her appeal-
ing letter to Mr. Pickwick, that "this business was from
the very first fomented and encouraged and brought
about by these men," but this is not much; for the
view only occurs to her when her operations had completely failed and recoiled on her own head with such
disastrous result. The firm's business was to persuade
her that she had a good case, and the Jury's verdict
proved that she had. Had Mr. Pickwick given in
and paid, she would have had no scruples. One cannot,
at the same time, but admire the ingenuity of the
author, in bringing such a Nemesis on her. Dodson
and Fogg, we are told, "continue in business from which
they realise a large income, and in which they are uni-
versally considered among the sharpest of the sharp."

At the last interview, at Perker's, when the costs were
paid, one might have expected Mr. Pickwick to behave
with a certain disdainful dignity. He was beaten and
had paid over the stakes, and could afford to treat his
enemy with contempt. Not so. The partners held out
the olive branch by alluding to the way they had passed
by his unmannerly attacks on them. "I beg to assure
you, sir, I bear you no ill will or vindictive feeling for

sentiments you thought proper to express of us in our office," and the other partner said, " I hope you don't think quite so ill of us, etc." This was rather gentlemanly and becoming. One offered his hand. But Mr. Pickwick broke out in a perfect fury. They had assumed a tone of forgiveness which was " an excess of impudence." He had been " the victim of their plots and conspiracies." They had imprisoned and robbed him. It was " insolent familiarity." At last he said, " *You are a well-matched pair of mean, rascally, pettifogging robbers.*" This sentence he repeated three times, and the words " Robbers " he shouted after them many times over the stairs.

Sharping attornies ! Why, a real sharping firm would have forced from their client advances of fee, " cash out of pocket," have made her give a Bill of Sale on her lease and goods, and have fairly stripped her of everything before the case began. Of the damages— had they got them—she would have seen but little.

The *Cognovit* that was extracted from Mrs. Bardell was an acknowledgement, as we have seen, which entitled them to enter up judgment just as if a trial had taken place. In the Oxford great Dictionary, it reads quaintly to find Mrs. Bardell's cognovit quoted as an illustration of the legal meaning.

The Turnkey, on her arrest, had told Sam that she had been brought to the Fleet, " on a Cognovit for costs," Sam imparted this news to Job Trotter, and sent him off, hot foot, to Perker in Montague Place. This outcast, was able to tell him, " it seems they got a *Cognovit* out of her for the amount of the costs, directly after the trial ! "

Boz, on this occasion, gives us a happy glimpse of Solicitor life. " Mr. Perker had a dinner party that day, which was certified by the lights in the drawing-room windows, the sound of an improved grand piano, and an improveable cabinet voice issuing therefrom ;

and a rather overpowering smell of meat which prevaded
the steps and entry. In fact, a couple of very good
country agencies happening to come up to town at the
same time, an agreeable little party had been got together to meet them, comprising Mr. Snicks the Life
Office Secretary, Mr. Prosee the eminent counsel, three
solicitors, one commissioner of bankrupts, a special
pleader from the Temple, a small-eyed peremptory
young gentleman, his pupil, who had written a lively
book about the law of demises, with a vast quantity of
marginal notes and references ; and several other eminent and distinguished personages. From this society
little Mr. Perker detached himself on his clerk being
announced in a whisper; and repairing to the dining-
room, there found Mr. Lowten and Job Trotter looking
very dim and shadowy by the light of a kitchen candle,
which the gentleman who condescended to appear in
plush shorts and cottons for a quarterly stipend, had,
with a becoming contempt for the clerk and all things
appertaining to 'the office,' placed upon the table.

'Now Lowten,' said little Mr. Perker, shutting the
door, 'what's the matter? No important letter come
in a parcel, is there?'"

Do we not seem to be present? We can never pass by
Russell Square without calling up the scene. Note, too,
the components of that legal dinner. Poor Sir F. Lockwood used to declare that he relished "Mr. Prosee, the
eminent counsel," more than any one of Boz's legal
circle. Yet these five words are all we know of him. But
Sir Frank had imagination, and like some of us could
read between the lines, or rather, between the words.
Here was a prominent member of the Bar—was he K.C.?
a triton among the minnows—therefore heading the
table, listened to with reverence as he told of the judges,
possibly of "old Stareleigh's" last exhibition of petu-
lance—" with it's high time for him to go, etc." But if

he had not silk, why did not Perker retain him instead
of the incapable Phunky, whom he did *not* ask on this
occasion. " I gave the chap a good chance, but he
destroyed my whole case ! " " Catch me letting him put
his legs under my mahogany." Among the guests was
that " small-eyed, peremptory young gentleman "—the
special pleader's pupil. What a capital sketch has Boz
given of him. " He had written a *lively* book about
the law of demises, with a vast quantity of marginal
notes and references." He had come with his teacher,
who was no doubt highly deferental to Mr. Prosee, but
enough, the peremptory young gentleman may have
partly " tackled " the great man on some point of practice. The good country agencies must have gone home
delighted with their evening.

But Mr. Prosee may be brought into somewhat closer
communication with the case. At Perker's dinner the
gentlemen had gone up to the drawing room, when Perker
was called down to hear the news of Mrs. Bardell's arrest.
Mr. Prosee was left expatiating to the circle on some
beautiful " point," and when Perker returned how likely
that he should tell of his extraordinary client who had
preferred to go to prison rather than pay the costs of a
suit, "and here," he would go on, " is the drollest sequel
you ever heard, &c."

" An odd unusual thing," Mr. Prosee would say.
" Plaintiff and Defendant, both in jail together ! I never
heard the like." There would be much laughter at the
novel situation. Thus the *cognovit* would come up
and Mr. Prosee gravely say, " nothing will be done
till an Act of Parliament is passed. The client should
be protected by a fresh solicitor." On which the young
author of the treatise on Demises would have something
to say in his best fashion ; for the *cognovit* might be
taken to be a sort of demise. " I doubt Mr. Prosee,
if your suggestion would work. As I take it, sir, etc.,"

RELEASE FROM THE FLEET.

But the circumstances connected with Mr. Pickwick's release from the Fleet, show the adroitness and ability of Dodson in a high degreee. It will be recollected that when Job rushed with the news to Perker, that gentleman and his clerk broke out into raptuous admiration.

"'Now, Lowten,' said little Mr. Perker, shutting the door, 'what's the matter? No important letter come in a parcel, is there?'

'No, sir,' replied Lowten. 'This is a messenger from Mr. Pickwick, sir.'

'From Pickwick, eh?' said the little man, turning quickly to Job. 'Well; what is it?'

'Dodson and Fogg have taken Mrs. Bardell in execution for her costs, sir,' said Job.

'No!' exclaimed Perker, putting his hands in his pockets, and reclining against the sideboard.

'Yes,' said Job. 'It seems they got a cognovit out of her for the amount of 'em, directly after the trial.'

'By Jove!' said Perker, taking both hands out of his pockets and striking the knuckles of his right against the palm of his left, emphatically, 'those are the cleverest scamps I ever had anything to do with!'

'The sharpest practitioners *I* ever knew, sir,' observed Lowten.

'Sharp!' echoed Perker. 'There's no knowing where to have them.'

'Very true, sir, there is not,' replied Lowten; and then both master and man pondered for a few seconds.

with animated countenances, as if they were reflecting upon one of the most beautiful and ingenious discoveries that the intellect of man had ever made. When they had in some measure recovered from their trance of admiration, Job Trotter discharged himself of the rest of his commission. Perker nodded his head thoughtfully, and pulled out his watch."

Now to the superficial this seemed to be evaded by the art of the firm in "getting the cognovit out of her," But this was an ordinary, vulgar stroke—which anyone could have done. Their policy went far deeper, and this Perker was acute enough to recognize. There was no object in putting Mrs. Bardell into the Fleet.

They could no more get their costs out of her, than they could get them out of Mr. Pickwick. She had nothing but her few "sticks" of furniture, worth say £50. But the astute fellows saw what pressure could be put on the benevolent nature of Mr. Pickwick, who could not endure that a respectable woman should be exposed to the contamination of a debtor's prison. And their sagacity was to be justified, and on the very next day, too.

It is curious, however, that no mention is made of Mrs. Bardell's release. It, of course, took place before Mr. Pickwick's. Here again Dodson and Fogg behaved very fairly, for they allowed both her and Mr. Pickwick to be released, without receiving payment, but simply on "an understanding" by Perker. As it turned out, indeed, they were not paid for some weeks.

The processes by which Mr. Pickwick was got into the Fleet were complicated enough, *Habeas Corpus*, appearing before functionaries, etc. But it is odd that in cases of persons of lower degree these seemed not to be necessary. We do not hear of them in Sam's instance. While Mrs. Bardell, was taken straight from "the Spaniards," to the prison door, she was not even formally arrested by the Bailiff, though he was in attendance. He sat afar off at Hampstead, taking his drink—and on the box during the drive. She might be said to have been arbitrarily taken to the prison by Jackson—without a legal warrant. Had not the business been compromised, some other astute firm of attorneys might have found subject for an action against Dodson and Fogg.

Another of the humorous incidents connected with the case is old Weller's firm persuasion that Mr. Pickwick was to " stand his trial," as though he were indicted for some criminal offence. We find him always astray as to when he was to be " tried," etc. This is a most natural impression among the lower classes, who are not very clear as to the distinction between civil and criminal process, being most familiar with the latter. In the same spirit is his humorous suggestion of securing an *alibi*, as the best method of getting Mr. Pickwick off. " O Sammy, Sammy, vy worn't there a alleybi ! "

Such is " The Trial in Pickwick."

Is there any writer, now living, I may be asked, who could furnish such a picture as this, one so full of reality and true humour, of one of our modern Courts of Justice ? The answer must be that it would be idle to look for such a person. There are thousands who could supply minute drawings in which not a single detail would be omitted. But the piercing to the essence, the happy generalization, the knowledge of the true points of character, these would be sought in vain.

www.ingramcontent.com/pod-product-compliance
Lightning Source LLC
Chambersburg PA
CBHW032006190326
41520CB00007B/374